Life-Writes

Where do Writers' Ideas Come From?

It's Called Life

Life-Writes

Where do Writers' Ideas Come From?
It's Called Life

Suzanne Ruthven

COMPASS
BOOKS

Winchester, UK
Washington, USA

First published by Compass Books, 2012
Compass Books is an imprint of John Hunt Publishing Ltd., Laurel House, Station Approach,
Alresford, Hants, SO24 9JH, UK
office1@o-books.net
www.o-books.com

For distributor details and how to order please visit the 'Ordering' section on our website.

ISBN: 978 1 84694 853 4

A CIP catalogue record for this book is available from the British Library.

Design: Lee Nash

Printed in the UK by CPI Antony Rowe
Printed in the USA by Edwards Brothers Malloy

CONTENTS

Introduction 1
Chapter One: Absence of Thought 3
Chapter Two: Standard Operating Procedure 16
Chapter Three: Exercise of the Intellect 31
Chapter Four: Looking From All Angles 42
Chapter Five: Innermost Thoughts 48
Chapter Six: Food For Thought 56
Chapter Seven: Lost in Thought 66
Chapter Eight: Ordeal By Fire 76
Chapter Nine: Writer's Itch 91
Chapter Ten: Dramatis Personae 101
Chapter Eleven: Cruise to Nowhere 113
Chapter Twelve: Have Them Rolling In The Aisles 125
Chapter Thirteen: Mirror of the Mind 136
Chapter Fourteen: Mother of the Muses: Mnemosyne 152
Chapter Fifteen: Token of Remembrance 160
Chapter Sixteen: Scraping the Bottom of the Barrel 170
Chapter Seventeen: Call Back Yesterday 183
Chapter Eighteen: Memory Lane 201
Chapter Nineteen: A Novel Idea 211
Chapter Twenty: Famous Last Words 229

Introduction

Suzanne Ruthven is the editor of the popular quarterly creative writing magazine, *The New Writer* (which she produces in partnership with literary agent, Merric Davidson). As well as providing a much-needed platform for new fiction and poetry on an international level, *TNW* contains features and interviews by experienced writers, with current news and views from the publishing world.

She started her professional writing career in 1987 by founding the small press writers' magazine, *Quartos,* which ran for nine years until its merger with *Acclaim* in 1996. In addition to acting as a judge for several national writing competitions, she has also tutored at writers' workshops including The Annual Writers' Conference (Winchester College), The Summer School (University of Wales), Horncastle College (Lincolnshire) and the Cheltenham Literature Festival. The original idea for the *From the Editor's Desk* workshops was taken from her creative writing book of the same name, with both proving to be highly popular with writers' groups. As a result of a successful series of workshops for The Welsh Academy, she was invited to become a full member of the *Academi* in recognition of her contribution to literature in Wales.

She is author of over 20 books on spiritual, country and self-help matters (including two novels and *Creative Pathways: Freeing the Writer's Inner Voice*) and has contributed articles to a variety of publications as diverse as *The Lady, The Countryman, Prediction* and the *Funeral Director's Journal* ; extending her literary interests still further in 1994 by founding ignotus press to market and promote new authors in the mind, body and spirit genre. For over 10 years the press was recognised as one of the leading publishers in the metaphysical genre, and remained so until her retirement and move to Ireland in 2007. Ruthven has also 'ghost written' numerous books for other writers in the metaphysical, country and folklore genre, including an autobiography for one of Britain's leading field sportsmen, which was nominated for the William Hill Sports Book of the Year in 2006. In 2011 she became commissioning editor for Compass Books, a writers' resource imprint for John Hunt Publishing.

Life-Writes is based on Suzanne Ruthven's inimitable tutoring style for her workshops, and as she says: *"I'm a commissioning editor for a publishing house and a magazine editor, but first and foremost, I'm a writer, and so my allegiance is always going to be with serious writers who want to see their work in print."*

Chapter One

Absence of Thought

"Within the space of fifteen minutes, the horse escaped from the paddock and went down with colic ... two swallows flew into the cottage and got trapped in the sitting room ... three large dogs pitched in to help expel the invaders ... and in the midst of all this mayhem, the magazine deadline was looming ..."

The second most common question a writer is asked, is 'where do your ideas come from?' [The first is: 'Do you make any money from it?'] Experienced writers don't go looking for ideas; ideas come to them. An experienced writer just has the knack of spotting what makes a good story (in this case, an editorial) ... or what will make a good story once it's been given the right spin ... because none of us, if we're honest, will let reality get in the way of a saleable piece of work.

The opening dramas really did happen, but they took place over several hours without any of the fauna involved suffering adverse side effects. The horse had an injection; one swallow escaped without help, while the other required an open window before it made its exit. The greyhounds had a Bonio apiece and went back to sleep; and *The New Writer* was duly despatch via **www.mailbigfile.com** on schedule. Condense the story into a 15-minute drama and it gives a thumb-nail sketch of the hectic domestic life of a freelance writer and editor. Tell it like it really was and the reader response would be: 'So what!'

All editors are looking for an element of action, drama or surprise, even in non-fiction. It's what catches their attention and makes them pause to read further; and the key to any editor's heart is originality. Not necessarily a new departure in style or genre, but a refreshing and original slant on a popular theme. The writers whose work has been accepted for publication, managed to spark the editor's interest because those particular typescripts stood out from the rest on a dull, wet Monday morning.

It's not always easy to be objective about our own work, but the first question we need to ask is: why did those other writers stand out? What was so special about that particular piece of writing? What made the editor decide to published them over the hundreds of others (including our own submission) arriving in the office during that month?

- It may have been brilliantly written – but so are hundreds of others.

- It was probably topical – but so are hundreds of others.

- It probably met every point in the contributors' guidelines – but so did hundreds of others.

The answer, without doubt, was that particular writer's approach to a common or popular theme was so fresh and appealing that it was almost as if the editor was reading about the subject for the first time. In other words – **originality**!

One of the first instructions I usually give at a writers' workshop is to always discard the first idea that comes into your head. And while you're at it, discard the second … and third idea, too. This is because a hundred other writers will have had an identical thought for an article (poem or short story) stimulated by something seen on television, read in a magazine or newspaper, or heard on the radio. We may not consciously realise that this has been the source of our inspiration but the seed has been planted firmly in the deep recesses of the brain.

In fact, running the annual *TNW* Prose & Poetry Prizes we can usually predict the predominant theme(s) for competition entries and, more often than not, the approach to the subject itself, will also be repetitive. Here the only difference between a good and bad submission is the standard of writing and use of language. And the thing that makes a submission stand apart from the rest is where the writer has thought outside the box and developed the idea laterally. Linear thinking rarely wins prizes or editorial selection.

Let's say, for example, that a national scandal has erupted in the news involving key players in the horseracing world, and the question is raised as to whether they will be present at Aintree some months down the line. You may have a passion for the gee-gees and think that there will be a market somewhere for a piece on the Grand National ... but so will hundreds of other writers. The collective subconscious has been busy and already thousands of fingers will be busy typing out a history of the race, with or without a list of past runners and riders.

Stop and think for a moment: The editor of *The Racing Post*, won't be interested; top equestrian magazines such as *Horse & Hound* will have seen it all before, and publications aimed at other horsey disciplines will not be featuring a historical article on the 'sport of kings'. Unless you're a known name in sporting journalism, it's doubtful whether any of the top trainers or jockeys will be willing to talk to you; and unless you have some fabulous, previously unpublished racing photographs of Royalty, there's little scope for anything by a freelance.

Or is there ... several ideas spring immediately to mind:

- The groundsman responsible for the maintenance of the hallowed turf, or all-weather track, providing an interview doesn't infringe on race day and you are capable of asking intelligent questions.

- The private owner is always good for a story – like the couple who had a runner in the 2010 Grand National, which they kept stabled on their allotment!

- Work riders and/or stable staff grow very attached to their charges and although you won't get any inside information on the horses, there's scope for a career piece on what it takes to work in a busy racing yard.

- Ladies' Day sees the women competing for the best-dressed prize and some fashion tips on how to jazz up an existing outfit for the occasion might appeal to a fashion editor in these times of recession. Exactly what *do* you wear for a race meeting?

- Everyone is interested in food these days and an insight into the catering arrangements provided for the hospitality suites, with suitable adaptations for home cooking might just make an editor's mouth water. Find out the name of the caterer and obtain some sample menus if no one is available to talk to you.

- Former apprentice jockey Jim Anderson turned his hand to poetry and paid this homage to the great dual Derby winner and 1981 champion, who was stolen from his stable by the IRA and never seen again, after their demands for ransom were refused.

SHERGAR

So that was it old friend. So much for men.
The Crowns and laurels count for nothing now
And those who came like sneak-thieves in the night,
Have Cain's eternal mark upon their brow.

They did their master's bidding; made their name;
Not as you did in battle's glorious fire.
No courage, spirit, heart or talent asked.
Just worthless souls which cheaply were for hire.

Reprinted by the kind permission of SportsBooks Limited of Cheltenham
Shergar & Other Friends: An anthology of horseracing poetry

Added to that, there are several possible target markets here that wouldn't normally be interested in horseracing, including regional magazines if there is a local connection. Equine publications aimed at the young rider might accept a career article, even though they may not usually feature horse racing. Women's magazines could feature an Aintree, Ascot, Kentucky Derby or Melbourne Cup luncheon for the ladies, while the men are glued to the television, or off watching the race. Trade or professional papers catering for park-keepers and groundsmen might consider an interview with the man responsible for keeping the course looking good. And even if you miss Aintree, there are dozens of premier race meetings taking place all over the world, throughout the year that might adapt themselves to this kind of spin.

⇨ **Learn to think outside the box.**

The Reference Shelf

Few of us can keep facts, figures and dates in our head and this is where a good reference library comes in handy. All writers need reliable reference books in addition to a good Dictionary and Thesaurus, and it's not a bad idea to include those we can pick up and flick through in idle moments to spark off an idea for a story, poem or article. We glance at a page ... a phrase or quotation jumps out ... and an idea is born. Here are a few recommendations for old favourites that can still suggest new ideas:

> *Brewer's Dictionary of Phrase & Fable.* Originally printed in 1870, the updated version still contains words that have passed out of the language and gives a fresh insight into familiar phrases.
>
> *Chambers Book of Days: A Miscellany of Popular Antiquities in connection with the Calendar.* The original was published in 1864 but the revised edition can provide endless scope for seasonal material.
>
> *The Oxford Names Companion,* the definite guide to surnames, first names and place names of the British Isles.
>
> *The Penguin Guide to the Superstitions of Britain & Ireland* by Steve Roud, was the first new survey in over a generation to provide fresh insight into common superstitions.

Keep these books on your desk and open a page at random while you're having coffee. The next thing you know, there is the germ of interest in the creative recesses of the brain and you want to know more. Keep a pack of yellow 'post-it' notes handy and mark the page for a return visit.

⇨ **Reference books are the writer's life blood**

What the How-To Books Don't Tell You

Since creative writing became one of the largest growth industries in the hobbies market, there have been countless how-to books written advising new writers on the best way to get their work into print. So here's a simple A-Z checklist of some of the do's and don'ts to get out of the way before we start:

Agent

A semi-mythical creature that inhabits the twilight world of publishing. Everyone seeks them but they remain elusive and shy, avoiding new and not-so-new writers like a cat avoids water. Can only be attracted by the smell of success ... when the writer has already hooked a publisher's interest ... after the author has done all the work.

Book

The Holy Grail of all publishing ambition and a must-have for all serious writers, both old and new. If unable to place the typescript with a mainstream or small, independent publisher, many writers go for self-publication, regardless of the cost or quality of the content.

Clichés

A no-go area according to the how-to books but they form an integral part of our daily speech, are easily identifiable, and appear constantly as the basis for hundreds of titles in magazines. If uncomfortable with using an old-fashioned cliché – invent your own.

Discipline

Try to write something every day during a set time period. Great idea in a perfect world. Most households don't function like that and it is almost impossible to set aside a daily creative period when football is on TV; the cat's just been sick on the mat, or the dog needs to be rushed to the vet; a child has found an exciting new way of attempting to eliminate itself; and the boiler's packed in. Self proclaimed discipline is a smug person's way of letting you know that they're a more serious writer than you are.

Email Submissions

Easy to lose and/or ignore. Not always viewed as serious contact if the office is busy and can therefore be deleted with a flick of the little finger. *Whoops!* Make sure this is an acceptable means of contact before submitting your work via this medium.

Frustration

A permanent condition that hampers a writer's every attempt to get things done. Like trying to get some sense out of the 'girl on the switchboard' when you're trying to find out the correct editor to whom you wish to send your material. The jury is still out on whether she's being deliberately awkward, or just plain thick.

Good Advice

Ignore it! As Oscar Wilde said: *"I always pass on good advice. It is the only thing to do with it. It is never any good to oneself."* But still lots of it around, and everyone's an expert on getting published these days.

Humour

An absolute minefield for the fledgling writer. Never state that you are submitting a humorous piece as ten to one it will fail to amuse the editor. If they read it and it makes them laugh, it's humour and stands by itself - telling an editor they are about to be amused seldom works. Most humour pieces that arrive on an editor's desk usually mean instant rejection, simply because they don't even raise a chuckle.

Ideas

Let's get one thing straight - there's no such thing as an original idea in publishing. *"Ahhh!"* I hear you cry. *"What about Harry Potter?"* Been done before ... what about all those Enid Blyton boarding school adventures? It's a highly original slant on an old (and in its time, very popular) theme. JKR had the imagination to extend that theme into the world of fantasy and came up with a winner. And that's exactly what we're talking about!

Jam on the Bread

In other words, getting paid for your work. OK ... agreed it's exciting to see your byline in the initial stages of a writing career but just how long are you willing to carry on churning out material for free? How-to books will guide the novice towards a diversity of publications but hardly ever state that very few of the mags listed will stump up with cold, hard cash in return for your well-crafted piece. Expecting to earn a living from the written word is a very precarious situation indeed.

Karma

Or putting it another way, 'don't piss off the editor'. Editors move around from mag to mag or between publishing houses - and have *very* long memories, so any altercation may single out a writer as a person who's too much trouble to deal with. This isn't to say that all editors are good guys, but your 'trouble' may still come back to haunt you several years down the line.

Letters

Accompanying letters need to be short, concise and to the point, rather than some rambling discourse that gives everything from your blood group to your grandmother's maiden name. This style of letter may just convince an editor, agent or publisher that they couldn't possibly work with you, no matter how much they might like your work.

Muse

A pretentious referral to some perceived guardian/creative angel, who hasn't got anything better to do, other than sit around feeding ideas to wannabe writers. Also used as an excuse for not writing, because the creative Muse has gone AWOL (see **Writer's Block**).

No Word Count

All magazine submissions, both fiction and non-fiction, have to fit into a slot in the publication's layout. If this information isn't included on the title page you risk having your otherwise excellent piece being discarded because everyone's too busy to sit down and work out whether it's going to fit the pre-allocated space.

Opinions

Never have one! The majority of editors dislike 'opinion pieces', so if you want to make a political or controversial statement get quotes from both sides of the argument before you begin. The writer's voice is merely the channel for other people's viewpoints. A good journalist, however, can always get the intended message across by knowing when, where and how to use the quotes. Leave yourself out of the picture.

Publishers

The Olympians of the publishing industry are almost as difficult to corner as **Agents**. These lofty creatures aren't looking for the next Dan Brown or JKR, they're looking for someone *new*. No matter how good your presentation, there's got to be much more to catch their eye. Study publisher's catalogues and become familiar with the type of material they are looking for ... and try to pre-empt them!

Quirks and Foibles

Every editor has them ... silly little things that please or annoy, which can lead to rejection as quick as [insert appropriate cliché or simile]. Quirks and foibles have little to do with the actual presentation of a typescript ... it's more to do with a writer's personal style. Twee address stickers … signature in pink ink …coloured/fancy paper ... spelling a name incorrectly ... Don't leave yourself open to an editor's personal dislikes by not submitting a totally professional package.

Rejection Slips

Possibly the most boring subject in the whole field of creative writing but the same old stories circulate about how many times [insert name of famous writer of your choice] had a MS rejected, together with personal tales of having received enough rejection slips to paper the lavatory. Every writer receives rejection slips ... just the same as everyone receives an electricity bill. It's just not worth commenting on, never mind writing tedious articles about them.

Stamped-Addressed Envelopes

There has been a great deal of speculation over the fate of the SAE in publishing circles. Often comes under the same heading as 'Where do flies go in the winter?' No matter how many SAEs a writer encloses with submissions, there is very little chance that the 'girl in the office' will be able to marry a SAE to a submission, so no chance of a reply. And you do have to stick the right amount of stamps on if you want a reply, because SAE means 'stamped-addressed' not self-addressed envelope. And IRC means International Reply Coupon.

Typing

Nice old-fashioned concept in this age of computers but you'd be surprised how many experienced writers don't observe the basic rudiments of the typing class. Such as changing the 'ribbon' (i.e. ink cartridge) when printing off a finished typescript. Editors still receive pale (and therefore not interesting), single-spaced sheets that are extremely difficult to read, and often from experienced writers who should know better.

Under Pressure

Professional writers are always under pressure. Once you have your proposal accepted, whether for a full-length book, magazine feature or regular column in a local newspaper, you will be under pressure to supply on time. Once you miss that deadline the opportunity will be gone and someone else will step in. This is why it is essential to understand that it's not a good idea to give up the day job if part-time writing finances your living expenses. The pressures on a writer are great enough without having to worry about the mortgage, paying off the car, or covering the monthly direct debits.

Vulneratus Non Victus

Literally meaning 'wounded but not conquered' and an ideal motto for a beginner writer. Beware of using foreign words and phrases without clarification, otherwise you'll come across as trying to be too clever.

Writer's Block

One of the most popular urban myths of all. Only amateurs refer to it as though it is some form of obligatory childhood complaint such as chicken pox or measles - professional writers can't afford to have it, and don't get it. They work on something else until the ideas start to flow again.

X-Factor

The sign that all the chemicals have blended well enough to turn dross into gold. It can't be defined but everyone can recognise it when they read it. Aim to give the performance of a lifetime but don't be too devastated if someone else is declared the winner. When all is said and done, the final decision will always go to the item that appeals personally to the editor or competition judge.

Yearbook

Every writer has their favourite version but do bear in mind that a lot of information can be out of date before publication comes around. This is because yearbooks are compiled a year in advance, so all details should be checked before submitting material.

Zany

Can be initially appealing but wears thin after a while. Use in your writing but not in your covering letter to an editor. Keep these do's and don'ts in mind and, with an added emphasis on originality, we're ready to pursue another shy and elusive creature, the commissioning editor.

> **Handy Hint:**
> When submitting non-fiction, amateur offerings are usually conspicuous by the lack of anecdotes, quotes, original material and/or human interest ... and often read as though most of the details have been lifted verbatim from a guide or text book. Make sure anything submitted for consideration has the right balance of the above, with a bit of human-interest for good measure.

Try This Exercise:

Be adventurous! Don't be afraid to step outside your normal target market. It's easy to stay in a 'safe zone' and keep submitting to the same outlets but you always need to be on the lookout to expand your own marketplace. And don't overlook the foreign magazines – many of which are aimed at English-speaking readers.

- Make a point of submitting something completely different to new magazines – i.e. articles instead of fiction – at least once a month.

- Make sure you are familiar with the new readership and keep a strict record of where each piece has been sent.

Chapter Two

Standard Operating Procedure

Basically there are
Two kinds of people,
Those who are creative
And those who are destructive:
And the latter are more operative.
Gwyn Thomas, National Poet of Wales

Having edited a writers' magazine for over 20 years, and acted as commissioning editor for a small, independent publisher for a decade, I think it's safe to say that generally speaking, most submissions are rejected because the writer has:

- had an idea, and not bothered to develop it into something out of the ordinary.
- not attempted to find the right marketplace.
- completely ignored the submission guidelines.
- not made a study of other publications on the back list, or previous issues of the magazine

If it hadn't been for indulging in a bit of serious market research one wet Irish afternoon, none of my three non-fiction books would have been under contract by the end of 2010. *"Who's the most popular publisher for my sort of stuff, these days?"* I asked a friend who runs one of the more interesting bookshops in London. She gave me two names. The first, and despite the rather uninspiring entry in *The Writer's Handbook,* I went to the website ... made a telephone call and 48 hours later I had the emailed contract in my possession! Two months later I had the contract for a second book. The other publisher mentioned has never bothered to respond. In all fairness there had been a change of commissioning editor and that *may* have accounted for the silence. I *may* try them again when I have written something else that suits their list … but then again, I may not.

The third book was sold to a publishing company who does not appear in any of the writers' handbooks, and neither does its sister publishing venture, a monthly magazine. Another friend who advertises in the magazine told me to have a look at it for a possible article outlet. In trawling through the website I discovered the link for books and back issues ... and five weeks later the contract for *Signposts For Country Living* was signed and sealed, and the first part of the advance paid.

⇨ **Don't rely on existing sources to provide you with a marketplace – go out and find your own.**

The Writer's Diary

The moral of this story is that although writers' handbooks list hundreds of publications, there are much wider publishing opportunities that do not always appear in these hallowed pages. If you have a specialist subject, it might pay to do as I did and check through trade or professional publications governing that subject, or ask people with similar interests: *"Which publisher or magazines do you read/recommend?"*

My experience as a commissioning editor has also shown that writers will work through A-Z of the handbooks, regardless of whether their material is compatible with the publisher's guidelines. They literally start at 'A' and send proposals to every publishing company listed — even when the entry states quite categorically that the publisher does not want to receive the type of material they're proposing. I am aware that I've banged on *ad nauseaum* over the years about the importance of market research, but it's still as vital as ever, if not more so, in today's computerised publishing climate. Especially as I now have a sneaking suspicion that many smaller publishers deliberately *don't* include their details in the handbooks, and thus avoid having to deal with hundreds of unsolicited typescripts from unreasonable people.

We should also be aware that time and publishers' fads wait for no writer, and that books appearing in the shops and literary supplements in July, were contracted up to 18 months previously. And usually the bigger the publisher, the longer the wait for the book to be produced. Of course, it isn't possible to second guess what publishers see as next year's potential bestsellers, but there will be little point in submitting a proposal for what was being commissioned 18 months previously. Like all areas of business, publishing trends move fast, and as authors we need to use more than just our imaginations to get ahead of the game.

- Begin by making a list of all the publishing houses that accept titles in your genre, and make a point of regularly logging onto their respective websites to check for forthcoming titles and up-and-coming authors.

- Set time aside each month to devote to updating your potential market outlets and discover the subtle differences between each publisher's requirements – regardless of where you live in the world!

A writer's income derives from material sent out weeks, months, or even a year, previously and so there needs to be a continuous stream of work under consideration and/or acceptance to provide a regular financial return. A large proportion of freelancers earn considerably less than £4000 per year from their writing alone, and the competition gets fiercer with each passing year. Which is why it is said that professional writing is roughly 60% forward planning and 40% talent; and why successful writers always work with an eye on the calendar, not the clock.

For example: As I sit here wondering what to write about in the next magazine editorial, the sun is shining and bathing the Galtee mountains in a misty blue autumnal haze. It's the weekend that the clocks alter. By the time our subscribers read about it, we will have been plunged into the gloom that usually follows the festive season and my mountain view will probably be shrouded in dense fog and darkness. January and February are gloomy months but the writer can't afford the New Year blues ... if you're not already doing it, resolve to send out one proposal or submission per week. Needless to say, much depends on career/domestic commitments but you should soon be able to increase your target to two or even three proposals/submissions per week once you get into the habit.

I appreciate that it's often difficult to conjure up images of summer in the middle of winter, or offering new ways to celebrate Christmas around Midsummer Day but that's exactly what editors are doing. Any seasonally themed piece, whether fact or fiction, needs to be submitted some 6-12 months ahead of the publication date. And, at risk of repeating myself, there needs to be an original slant on the traditional offerings, not the same tired old 'how to survive Christmas/summer holidays with relations' etc. This is why *Chambers Book of Days: A Miscellany of Popular Antiquities in connection with the Calendar* is such a 'must-have' because it acts as a great seasonal reminder, and focuses the attention on distant points in the calendar with a flick of the pages.

⇨ **Don't get left behind ... plan ahead.**

The writer-editor relationship

Most writers begin their careers by submitting material to magazines, and providing we comply with all the editorial guidelines, it is easy to build up a good working relationship with an editor that can often continue for many years. Editors are always looking for new talent and, with the exception of the monthly glossies that generally have a large in-house team for regular pieces, will usually respond favourably to a freelance enquiry.

Study several current issues before sending anything to the magazine. Websites often feature samples of back issues for a year or more, and this will tell you whether anything similar to your idea has recently been published. There is little point an editor repeating what has gone before and often a really good article will be rejected purely for that reason. Editors of magazines are more likely to give words of encouragement on the rejection slip and, if they like your work, will usually say so. If this happens, it's advisable to submit something else as quickly as possible.

Unfortunately, it's becoming more and more usual for editors to sit on unsolicited articles indefinitely, and recently I've had two responses from completely different monthly magazines (one MB&S and the other a dog mag) where the editor states: *"I'll keep this on file in case I want to use it in the future."* Sorry … no! If an editor hasn't responded within a month, then the article is revamped and submitted elsewhere. There's no point in waiting around while an editor hedges his (or her) bets, and often the piece will be out of date, if we have to wait six months for them to make up their up mind. Having said that, the editor of *The Countryman* explained that he was working nearly 12-months ahead, and would I mind if my article was held back for publication until the autumn. Of course not …

A good magazine editor knows what they want for the readership and should be able to make a decision reasonably quickly. This is why it's better with non-fiction to send a proposal letter outlining the subject matter, approach and the reason why you are 'qualified' to write about it, but if an editor likes your work and you write for them regularly, don't allow yourself to become complacent. Keep sending material to other outlets because you never know when there will be a change of editor - and the new one might want to make changes that don't include you!

Needless to say, every magazine has its very own style and a writer needs to be mindful of the subtle differences that make a reader prefer one weekly magazine to another. An article tailored for and rejected by one publication will need some tinkering before it is sent off to another – although on first reading both magazines appear to be almost identical. And do resist the urge to carpet-bomb all the women's magazine with the same article – it doesn't work that way.

Lastly, always make a point of mentioning a fee when submitting, i.e. *"I enclose my article for consideration at your usual fee ..."* This tells the editor that you expect to be paid for your work. And it wouldn't be the first time I'd had a very prompt response stating that the magazine doesn't pay for contributions.

⇨ **Magazines and newspapers are the first step for professional writers.**

The writer-agent relationship

It has often been said that it is more difficult for a writer to be admitted to an agent's client listing than to gain acceptance by a publisher. A slight exaggeration perhaps, but there are even more writers seeking agents today than ever before. Creative writing has exceeded boom-time and statistics claim that one in five adults have written, or intends to write, a novel. Rather than attempt to answer the unanswerable with patronising waffle – 'How do I find an agent?' let's try to examine the literary agent's function in the publishing world from both the agent's and the writer's viewpoint.

Firstly, and most importantly, from the writer's position, it's a good idea to understand exactly what you're trying to sell and to whom. Literary agencies fall into two main categories - the big guys and the little guys. The big guys employ legions of staff to sort through typescripts; the little guys work solo, usually having left one of the bigger companies (either an agency or publishing house) to go it alone. Make sure you have a clear idea in your own mind about the kind of book you have written. If an agency states that it handles 'all types of books including children's ... good for crime and romantic fiction ...' followed by a recognisable selection of names from its client list, then your family saga/thriller might sit comfortably on their list. On the other hand, it's pointless submitting a good old-fashioned 'bodice ripper' to the agency that specialises in contemporary literary fiction.

The broader the speciality list, the larger the agency - and greater the number of staff to sell your book. This does mean, of course, that the sale needs to be financially viable, and so the bigger agencies are less likely to take on new writers - unless they're 99% sure there's a potential best-seller in the offing. Although media coverage of £150,000 advances for first-time novelists is an enticing carrot for wannabees, this sort of initial financial result is few and far between.

The writer-agent relationship is still a personal affair but should a new author be taken on by one of the bigger groups, it should be borne in mind that regular staff turnovers may mean that the agent with whom you have established a rapport may suddenly leave without warning. Although smaller agencies do not have the resources to give a book 100% attention (and, more often than not, will concentrate their efforts on the existing client list that earns them a living), they may be more sympathetic to new writers because they have fewer overheads and can risk the odd gamble if they like the look of a writer's work.

Do make sure, however, that the one-man-band has the right pedigree, i.e. genuine publishing experience, and beware of those who charge exorbitant reading fees as a prerequisite for taking on your book. Many agencies are now charging a reading fee, which is fine if the amount is reasonable and the response constructive, but also beware of any lack of professionalism in presentation and approach. For example, at ignotus press I received a proposal from someone claiming to be an agent except that the two-page accompanying letter explaining why they thought we'd be interested in their client's work, revealed that they hadn't bothered to check on what type of books we published. Added to that, the client's sample chapters were single-spaced ... and the synopsis droned on for five pages. The first question that sprung to mind was, had this 'agent' ever seen the inside of a publishing house?

Whatever the would-be novelist believes, no agent - large or small - can work miracles if the typescript isn't good enough. Neither does an agent have any room to manoeuvre if the author has already submitted the typescript to every publisher in the writers' handbooks. Repeated rejection might suggest that a professional assessment is required, and agents aren't in the business of giving a creative writing lesson on why it wasn't suitable, so please don't expect it.

Most agents are specific about what they will, and will not accept - and instructions are perfectly clear about submissions. If you choose to ignore these important details in the vague hope that you can buck the system, please don't send letters of complaint to all the writing magazines bemoaning the fact that you haven't had a response. The main reason for authors wanting or needing an agent usually hinges on the fact that publishers' readers are more likely to read a submission that has already been vetted by an agency. This indicates that there is a good storyline, the writing is competent and the agent is satisfied that there is a reasonably professional approach to the business of writing. So, whomever you choose to target, please, do be professional in your initial approach. All an agent needs to know in the opening stages is whether the writer can write and sustain the plot throughout the typescript, which should be evident from a well-written synopsis and three opening chapters.

More often than not, an agency has little time for niceties and typescripts are usually returned with a standard rejection slip. Judging from letters sent to us at *The New Writer*, writers resent this apparently casual dismissal of what can represent years of work but another thing to remember is that agents, by token of the business they're in, can afford to be extremely selective over accepting clients. The agency's first obligation is to its existing clients and doesn't have the facilities (or inclination) to act as a 'freebie' advice bureau.

⇨ **If you do get any words of advice or encouragement from an agent, treat them like gold even if they are brief.**

The writer-publisher relationship

Trying to sell a first novel is an extremely difficult business - even if it does happen to be brilliant. It was once an old school of thought that a well-written first novel would have a good chance of finding its way into print. Publishers may like, even love, a novel but if they can't find a slot for it then there will be no offer to publish. The perfectly crafted little gem may now have to wait a lot longer.

A new novelist may find it a little easier to get a foot in the door with the growing number of smaller, independent publishers rather than the mainstream conglomerates, since the smaller houses may also be willing to take more risks with a new author. This approach still needs thorough market research on the author's part, however, since there are still too many writers submitting proposals to publishers who are not (and never have been) interested in their particular line of writing. Non-fiction publishers also receive their fair share of fiction. True it is a well-publicised fact that publishers' readers *are* more likely to look favourably on a submission that has been submitted via an agent, but this is by no means a hard and fast rule. A first novel, professionally presented with a well-written synopsis and gripping opening chapters isn't going to be turned down because it's been written by an unknown, and not submitted via a literary agency.

But let's imagine that a publisher has liked what he's seen and agrees to take you on. If you have an agent then all the financial transactions will be dealt with on your behalf; if you're doing it alone, you need to be especially careful when it comes to signing the contract. There are all sorts of legal black holes that can swallow an author whole, so it may be worthwhile joining The Society of Authors. The Society provides a free contract advisory services for its members and is looked upon as the 'authors' union' - acting on the author's behalf when publishers don't uphold their end of the agreement.

Another point to remember is that the newly accepted writer has very little or no say in what happens to their book once the contract has been signed. The author will be expected to make certain amendments to the text; for the first timer these will often be 'non-negotiable' since she or he doesn't have the clout to be inflexible over matters of commercial or editorial policies, and may even discover that the option to publish has been withdrawn if they create too many difficulties.

For the first-time novelist, publisher's advances will more realistically be in the region of £500 -£2,000 - with payment being made in three, or sometimes, four stages. What we should never lose sight of is the fact that for the writer, the publication of their book is the culmination of years of tears, frustration and desperation: to the publishing company it is merely the production of another marketable commodity. Another aspect that has altered over the years is the turnover of publishing staff, so again, your original editor may not even be around to share a celebratory lunch. In fact, the author may be involved with three or more different editors before the actual book launch.

Having illustrated a thoroughly gloomy picture of the author's lot, there is, of course, the plus side. There is nothing to equal the thrill of receiving that first copy through the post in advance of the publication date. It's there in hardback (or paperback) and it really doesn't matter if you don't like the cover design - ***it's yours***. The product of years of re-writing, editing and rejection - and if you don't sit on the bottom step of the stairs and have a jolly good howl after the postman's left, I'd be very, *very* surprised. But it doesn't stop there - you will be a very rare author indeed who has been taken on, on the strength of one book alone. By the time the hardback version of your first book sees the light of day, your publisher will be expecting you to have almost completed the second.

Knuckling down to the second book has a cathartic affect in that it provides the determination to prove to yourself that your first success wasn't a fluke. It is difficult to concentrate on a completely different book when you still have remaining anxieties about the first, but this is what separates the professional sheep from the goats. The second book also brings about a different set of problems. The first was written in your own time and at a pace you had set. The second time around you are working to publishing deadlines with an editor nagging you for progress reports. They also might want to see sample chapters, which could get torn to shreds and disrupt your writing flow as they nit-pick over the plot ...

➪ **Remember you wanted to be a writer and writing is a very serious business.**

Dear Editor, Sir or Madam, or 'To Whom It May Concern'!

Believe it or not, those few words can be the kiss of death to any submission. Without reading any further it indicates that the writer hasn't bothered to check whether their work suits the house style of that particular magazine or publishing list. Again, they have probably selected their target from one of the writers' handbooks and blithely sent off the typescript without a second thought.

As we've seen, staff change quite frequently and it is advisable to read an up-to-date issue of the publication in case there have been any important changes since you last saw a copy. Incoming editors will impose their own personality on a magazine, and that may alter the whole slant of what will be required in the future, as happened when Rachel Johnson took over at *The Lady*. Conversely, if you didn't get on with the former editor, it's always worth trying to get a foot in the door with the new one if your approach is stylised to suit the new guidelines.

Publishing houses may also have different editors for different genres, and so 'Dear Sir or Madam' letters will land up in the slush pile or rubbish bin, simply because no one knows who to give them to! The person who opens the post hasn't got time to read through a proposal letter and make a studied decision as to who gets it – and even if they do, it may not be the correct editor. As a result, your submission has been a complete waste of time and money – especially if you've made the grave error of submitting an unsolicited, full-length typescript.

⇨ **You've written the piece, prepared a good submission package ... now make the call and find out who the right person is to read it. Don't spoil your chance by writing 'Dear Sir or Madam ...'**

Multiple & Simultaneous Submissions

Finally, a word about multiple and simultaneous submissions. The only instance when it's permissible to make multiple submissions is for poetry, when editors will often request that writers send up to six poems at a time. Send two or three unsolicited short stories or articles in the same envelope and they will probably go straight in the bin.

The question of simultaneous submissions is a lot more complex, so let's use an analogy before we start. Just suppose a market gardener was told that he could only sell one box of lettuce to Tesco or Wal-Mart at a time; and that these would have to be sold and eaten before he could sell another box to another supermarket chain. It wouldn't make for good business and his stock would be well past its sell-by date by the time he could offer it elsewhere. The same applies to writers' submissions.

Some editors state quite openly that it can take between 3-6 months before they will give a decision, so what are our options?

- All submissions should be tailored-made for the appropriate market and shouldn't automatically suit another editor's requirements. All typescripts would need some tinkering before being sent to another editor, so simultaneous submissions are not a good idea from the writer's point of view.

- By rule of thumb, give short stories, poems and articles a month before offering them elsewhere. Novels and non-fiction book proposals should be given between six to eight weeks before sending them off to the next publisher/agent on your list. Give them the courtesy of another six weeks to respond.

- A 'perhaps' 'later' 'maybe' response is no good to a writer. Keep your options open by all means, but a piece isn't sold until you have a formal confirmation.

The 'no simultaneous submissions' rule was put in place over a decade ago by publishers and editors, and has become another of those urban myths within the creative writing industry. It's dog in the manger stuff and if you've been waiting for weeks, or even months, for a reply, then it's hardly 'simultaneous' if you decide to submit to someone else after a reasonable delay. If your submission is accepted, do send a polite letter to any editor who's 'kept it on file' and explain that the piece has now been sold. And thank them for their time. You never know when you want to submit to them again.

The only real no-no for simultaneous submissions is when submitting material for a writing competition. Because there is often a 3-6 month lapse between the competition being announced and the closing date, be prepared for your entry to be on-hold until after the judging process has taken place. Generally speaking, however, material entered for competition, particularly short stories, would not be the sort of fiction normally written for commercial publication, since it tends to be more adventurous and non-genre specific.

⇨ **Every submission should be tailor-made for its intended market.**

These are the few basic rules of dealing with editors, agents and publishers, and now that we've got them out of the way, we can settle down to finding out exactly what makes original, marketable writing that you can sell.

Handy Hint:
An essential writer's tool is the indispensable 'card index' (manual or computerised) that gives an accurate, up-to-date picture of to whom we've submitted our work – including competitions - together with when, where and how. We need to know at a glance where everything is, and how long before it can be considered 'free' to be sent out again. When we receive an acceptance, we then record the proposed publication date and the fee expected.

Try This Exercise:

Make a list of all the subjects about which you have a reasonable knowledge; then make a list of the subjects that interest you on a more informal level. My two lists would include, for example:

- Creative writing; greyhounds; country matters; folklore; 'mind, body and spirit'; metaphysics; astronomy and ancient Egypt.

- WWII, classic Japanese cinema, theatre, kitchen craft; gardening; ancient and medieval history; geology; horseracing.

When starting out on our writing career it is advisable to 'write about what we know' but as we become more confident, we can branch out into writing about what interests us. So far, I've had books and articles published on everything in my first list, and used the second list as background information for other works of fiction and non-fiction.

Chapter Three

Exercise of the Intellect

"Everybody walks past a thousand story ideas every day. The good writers are the ones who see five or six of them. Most people don't see any." **Orson Scott Card**

Having dispensed with the nuts and bolts side of creative writing, we are now going to study the intuitive, imaginative and off-beat aspects. We are going to explore what I've called:

Creative Pathways For Writers – the 10 Secret Steps

1. There are more ideas locked away in your unconscious mind than you could ever write about in a whole lifetime – but how can they influence your creative writing. **The secret is finding the key to access them.**

2. There is a story (article or poem) behind everything you encounter during your daily routine in both inner and outer worlds if you have the courage to experience and explore. **The secret is learning to look behind the obvious.**

3. No matter how mundane and/or familiar a scene, there are countless different angles from which to view it. **The secret is thinking 'sideways'.**

4. You are unique: no one can access the same experiences and memories, which means you have the ability to generate unique responses to situations. **The secret is knowing how to express yourself.**

5. Creative energy fuels creativity, so immerse yourself with creative images and stimulating art forms to give fresh ideas and ignite the creative flame. **The secret is tapping into whatever can unleash creative energy.**

6. Encourage the flow of creative energy from your unconscious mind through visualisation, meditation and relaxation. **The secret is drawing energy from other sources.**

7. Use your imagination when exploring other artistic mediums such as painting, sculpture, music, etc., because creativity is a state of mind. **The secret is allowing other influences to stimulate the creative impulse.**

8. Give your imagination free rein and open up your unconscious mind to the creative possibilities around you; if necessary do the opposite of what is considered the norm. **The secret is having the strength to dream.**

9. By connecting to your unconscious mind you can explore the wealth of universal memories of myth, fantasy and symbolism – but don't be embarrassed by your ability to travel to the 'hidden' world. **The secret is channelling your favourite childhood images.**

10. Certain images or symbols open the door to the collective unconscious; try working with these mind pictures to stimulate your creativity no matter how ridiculous or outrageous at the beginning.**The secret is focussing the mind on those things that will encourage creative energy.**

Freeing the writer's inner voice

Because *Life-Writes* is about drawing on submerged inner resources, it means that I've chosen to share many of my own private thoughts and family memories to illustrate many of the points made in the text. As a result, this has become a very personal book, because the examples, stories and anecdotes are real-life revelations, not fictional ones. Drawing on our inner reserves means that we have to be honest with ourselves about how much we are actually willing to give, or reveal, to a general readership in order to further our writing career. Where, we must ask ourselves, does reality end and creative writing begin?

The original idea for my book, *Creative Pathways: Freeing the Writer's Inner Voice,* came after reading *The Pillow Book of Sei Shonagon,* a sort of personal journal of a lady-in-waiting at the court of the Emperor of Japan towards the end of the 10th century AD. Today, a pillow book refers to an illustrated manual of erotic advice but Sei's book was a mixture of diary, gossip column and 'commonplace' book that showcased her literary observations off to perfection. History tells us that both her father and great-grandfather were both noted poets and scholars and, were Sei Shonagon alive today, she would probably be one of our leading literary lights. In this capacity, she can quite easily fill the role of ancestral spirit, or *kami,* of creative inner thought.

Unlike Julie Andrews' 'Favourite Things' from *The Sound of Music,* however, the 'things' that Sei Shonagon commented upon were not always pleasing. Nevertheless it is her wide-ranging observations that set the pattern for some of the exercises for my creative writing workshops, combining Zen-like word-pictures and contemporary commercial writing ambition in order to free the writer's inner voice. The age-old categories were Sei Shonagon's own – the 'things' in *Creative Pathways* were mine. For example:

***The Pillow Book*:**

Things that arouse a fond memory of the past

Dried hollyhock. The objects used during the Display of Dolls. To find a piece of deep violet or grape-coloured material that has been pressed between the pages of a notebook.

It is a rainy day and one is feeling bored. To pass the time, one starts looking through some old papers. And then comes across the letters of a man one used to love.

Last year's paper fan. Night with a clear moon.

Creative Pathways:
Things that arouse a fond memory of the past
A collection of old family photographs
Old theatre programmes
A particular piece of music
Wood smoke
The smell of hawthorn or bluebells in blossom

Here we have two collections of memories (or, from the writer's perspective 'ideas') that immediately spark very clear images in the mind's eye despite the fact that eleven centuries separate them.

➪ **Make a note of your 'things that arouse a fond memory of the past' in your Ideas Book**

Start an Ideas Book

In order to begin searching for the key to accessing these new ideas, we need to start on a practical level by keeping an Ideas Book. As **Secret Step One** tells us, there are more ideas locked away in our unconscious minds than we could ever write about in a whole lifetime. What we must discover is how they can influence our short stories, novels, poetry or non-fiction to the very best of our ability.

Instead of relying on memory, the Ideas Book should be used to record snippets of conversation, great one-liners, quotations, reference books, locations and characters. The aim of *Life-Writes* is to encourage you to open your ears and eyes, to view things differently with your mind and heart. In other words, to free the inner voice so that you're not afraid to trust your imagination and take a few risks with your writing. Become an observer and develop a willingness to see people and the world around you in a completely different light. By expanding those powers of observation, you will continuously build on the entries in your Ideas Book, which in turn will help you re-explore existing plots and themes, and generate new ones. Try to be honest but above all, do not be afraid to push against any restrictions imposed by current thinking or political correctness. No one is going to see your Ideas Book – its contents are for your eyes only.

To set the ball rolling, the first entry will be to give five examples of what *you* consider to be 'things that arouse a fond memory of the past' and here we need to reflect on why we consider them to be 'fond memories'. The items on my list will probably be far removed from those on yours, while you will probably be completely unmoved by those 'things' that are important to me. What we also need to consider is the way that language has been devalued and how some words can take on a completely different emphasis when used in contemporary conversation. We are talking about perspective or viewpoint, and this is where we begin to access those ideas that are locked away in our unconscious minds. So let's begin with …

A collection of old family photographs

Images of a life-style that can never come again because the people from that time, and who made it worth remembering, are all dead. The family home, long since demolished to make way for a ring road. Childhood recollections of summer holidays, and family mealtimes. Pet dogs. Days at the beach. Haymaking and harvest. A childhood friend with whom we still keep in contact.

Many of these 'fond memories' will re-surface throughout this book because we are writing from Life, and drawing on happenings that are unique to one person. Your first collection of 'things' will probably prompt some rather serious thoughts but even these can be extended and expanded to encourage you to plumb the depths of your own 'ideas' and explore their possibilities.

Keeping a record of your own 'things' in your own Ideas Book should eventually lead to dozens of ideas for fiction, articles or poetry but first we need to explore ways of making them exciting before turning them into submissions. On a day-to-day basis, our conscious brain registers the 'facts' or the most obvious impressions about a situation; for creative writing it is necessary to dig deep into the subconscious to locate the ideas that have been compressed into the brain's equivalent of a computerised 'zip-file'.

⇨ **Our past is a mine of good ideas for future use.**

Right-hand brain reserves

As with using a computer, firstly we need to understand where to locate these compressed ideas before we can release them. At the same time, a certain amount of personal analysis is needed to see whether we fall into the category of an 'efficient parrot' acting purely on the instructions of the creative writing tutorials, or whether we do, in fact, possess 'originality, curiosity and intellectual courage' to take risks with our writing.

For these answers, we have to access the part of our brain that governs each and everyone's creative and/or intuitive impulses – i.e. the right-hand side of the brain. This can probably be best described as thinking with the heart or 'gut reaction' and is something that we've all experienced at one time or another. This duality of thought often occurs when we've a decision to make. One half of us wants to go ahead and take a risk, while the other half tells us to hold back because we are not being rational or practical. This is what psychologists refer to as left-brain and right-brain thinking (although they often differ in opinion over which is which).

Generally speaking, left-brain thinking influences the way we tackle living in general, and the way we home-in on a particular problem or issue. As far as the writer is concerned, the left-brain is the part that instils discipline and focus, directs our market research, insists on records and accounts being kept. In other words the practical, nuts and bolts of everyday writing chores, which we need to do in order to keep some kind of control over what we write, why we are writing it, who we write for, when we do it, where we send it and how we're going to achieve it.

Right-brain thinking is less easy to define simply because this is the area of intuition, gut-reaction, creative impulse, illogical and lateral influences. Many erroneously believe this is exclusively a 'female' trait (male being more practical, unimaginative, etc,) but it should more accurately be described as androgynous, since genuine creativity transcends gender. The right-brain is the creative source that produces innovative ideas from the deep recesses of our subconscious but it needs left-brain influences to finish the job. The right-brain creates but it is the left-brain that moulds, shapes and refines the 'idea' into marketable material. Right-brain skips through the cerebral landscape with a 'hello, birds, hello trees, hello sky' frame of mind, while left-brain trails along patiently in its wake, picking up the thoughts and ideas to process into something sensible when the right-brain settles down for a snooze.

Left to its own devices, right-brain probably couldn't produce a saleable poem or short story if its life depended on it, simply because the initial idea is disjointed and unpolished. This is why it needs to work in tandem with the left-brain's analytical influence. On the other hand, if the left-brain tries to produce a poem or short story independently of the right-brain's influence the result, more often than not, appears contrived and lacking in depth, with unformed characters and an unconvincing plot.

⇨ **The emphasis on word-play, lateral thinking and visualisation in *Life-Writes* will, hopefully, help you to access those recesses of the brain that more practical, left-brain writing tutorials can't reach.**

On Your Own Patch

To become a truly creative writer we have to start to notice and register the world around us from different angles and perspectives. It may be that our own particular patch has become so familiar that we no longer register what is going on there on a day-to-day basis. Make time to walk a familiar route and take notice of:

- what is growing in front gardens;
- new building developments;
- people standing at the bus stop;
- trees in the park;
- changes in shop window displays

Make a conscious effort to register the gradual changes as flowers begin to bloom; the buildings near completion; different people stand at the bus stop at certain times of the day; the trees in the park altering their appearance through the seasons; and window displays rarely remain the same for very long.

Think about where you live now. Is it the same place where you grew up? If so, how has it changed? For better or worse? Did you move away from your childhood or teenage stomping ground? Try to define the differences. What we need to remember, of course, is that memory is deceitful and illusionary, so what we think we can recall, may be almost as fictional as the novel we're trying to write. How many times have you argued with an old friend or sibling over the way you both remember things from the past.

Train yourself to become more observant about the common everyday things that go on around you. Recall to mind the words of William Henry Davies's *Leisure*:

"What is this life if, full of care,
We have no time to stand and stare?"

As writers, we owe it to ourselves to make time to stand and stare; even if it's only to study the dress code, mannerisms and body-language of fellow travellers on the subway, train or bus to work.

⇨ **Always be on the look-out for useable ideas.**

Point of View

Surprisingly enough, viewpoint can make all the difference in the world to a good idea, but this isn't merely a question of swapping sides in an argument. Throughout this book, we will be looking at ways to improve creative thinking until, hopefully, like the fly's eye, you will have more viewpoints than you can possibly handle. From the narrative point of view we have:

- **First person** - where one character tells the story, using the first-person pronoun 'I'. Although this method gives immediate focus on people and actions, it can be extremely restrictive because a single character's perception can be very limiting when story-telling.

- **Second Person** – where the writer uses 'you', as if talking to someone. Not an easy method of writing narrative and extremely difficult for a first-time novelist. Not advisable for popular fiction. Often used in how-to and self-help books when imparting instructions.

- **Third Person** – the most common point of view where the writer refers to characters by name or uses s/he to tell the story. This gives us more flexibility since it tells the story from everyone's viewpoint.

Possibly the best example of conflicting viewpoint is the Japanese film, *Rashomon,* which tells the story of a brutal murder from the viewpoint of the bandit, the murdered man's ghost, his wife and a wood-cutter. Because each has something to hide, there are distortions in each of the accounts and, by the end of the trial, it is impossible to decide who really is telling the truth.

It's not just personal perspective that distorts viewpoint. Take six witnesses to an accident and half the time they can't even agree on the colour of the vehicles involved in the incident. As Sherlock Holmes comments to Watson in *A Scandal in Bohemia, "You see, but you do not observe."* The majority of us see things on a daily basis but more often than not, we cannot give a true and accurate description of them – even under oath! The writer, like Holmes, must learn to observe life and its happenings if it's going to be used as grist for our literary mill. Opposing viewpoints can often add that essential ingredient of conflict/drama to a piece of writing, so bear this in mind when constructing your plot.

Hopefully, the first chapters of *Life-Writes* will have shown that using other levels of consciousness as a 'tool' for enhancing creative writing is not an impractical theory. We are merely employing different methods of lateral thinking - without the jargon - that are aimed specifically at the writer of poetry, fiction and non-fiction. The secret is, of course, that there are no secrets, no magic formulae.

⇨ **As we work our way through the book we will explore the various methods of looking at life from different angles in order to enrich our writing.**

> **Handy Hint:**
> Always keep a small notepad handy for jotting 'things' down. Ideally have a couple on the go that fit easily into a bag or pocket. Don't delay in making a note of snippets of conversation, ideas for future investigation or character sketches – we think we can recall them later but we lose that spontaneous reaction and the 'thing' becomes stale.

Try This Exercise:
Using five of your own things that arouse a fond memory of the past, write the opening line(s) (not more than a paragraph) for each one as either pieces of fiction, articles or poems - or a combination of any of the three disciplines - focussing on the theme of fond memory. Keep your results in your Ideas Book, and come back to them at a later date with a view to developing them into a full-length piece. Out of the five 'things' try writing at least one:

- Article
- Short story
- Poem

Chapter Four

Looking From All Angles

"Research, like writing, is an individual, creative process. It cannot be 'taught'. In his quest for original material – and who does not dream of stumbling upon a cache of hitherto unknown, unpublished papers or the answer to a problem that has baffled scholars for generations? – the writer never ceases to learn." **Ann Hoffman, *Research for Writers***

Many budding writers lack the confidence to take the first step into the commercial market place because they feel it is impossible to produce something completely new that no one else has ever thought of before. But as we've already observed : there is no such thing as a new idea. Most creative ideas have been used before, over and over again. What we are looking for are innovative ideas, so let us return to the dictionary definition to find that innovation means: *To introduce alterations; to put forward novelties. To alter or change by the introduction of something new.*

This is what will give our work that spark of originality. In all honesty, even the most block-busting novel is only a variation on a familiar theme rather than ground-breakingly new. For an example: in an earlier creative writing book, *From An Editor's Desk,* I threw in the Polti Theory, which maintained that there were only 36 dramatic situations on which the writer of fiction can draw. By using single situations or several combinations, the basic theme of every story (long or short) ever told, written or devised can be summed up in the following list:

Supplication
Deliverance

Crime pursued by vengeance
Vengeance taken for kindred upon kindred
Pursuit
Disaster
Falling prey to cruelty or misfortune
Revolt
Daring enterprise
Abduction
The enigma
Obtaining
Enmity of kinsmen
Rivalry of kinsmen
Murderous adultery
Madness
Fatal imprudence
Involuntary crimes of love
Slaying of a kinsman unrecognised
Self-sacrifice for an ideal
Self sacrifice for kindred
All sacrificed for passion
Necessity of sacrificing loved ones
Rivalry of superior and inferior
Adultery
Crimes of love
Discovery of the dishonour of a loved one
Obstacles to love
An enemy loved
Ambition
Conflict with God
Mistaken jealousy
Erroneous judgement
Remorse
Recovery of a lost one
Loss of a loved one

Fifteen years later and still editing a creative writing magazine, I would add that most non-fiction and poetry submissions also fall into those categories. If you don't believe me, check out the theme of the major features or stories in any selection of magazines or newspapers and you'll find most of them are loosely based on one or more of the above.

If we remove the smokescreen of exotic locations or glamorous lifestyle, we will find that most of the plots used by our favourite writers are telling the same old stories, over and over again. The basic theme of murder, intrigue, adultery and chivalry are all there – they just have an innovative backdrop. Colin Dexter, the creator of Inspector Morse introduced us to the esoteric world of academe by casting his novels amongst the traditions and dreamy spires of Oxford University life; while Simon Raven did the same for Cambridge.

Dick Francis came up with his own original formula set amongst the racing fraternity where wealth frequently rubs shoulders with the lower echelons of society. Jilly Cooper moved from Wimbledon Common to the equestrian set, before turning her attentions on the international orchestral and art worlds, and has since moved on to horse racing. Ellis Peters went back to medieval Britain. While in the fantasy department, Tolkien created Middle Earth and J K Rowling, Hogwort's … and more recently Stuart MacBride sets his Logan McRae novels in gritty Aberdeen; the six Roy Grace thrillers by Peter James have Brighton as the base; while Donna Leon, an American expat who has chosen to relocate herself to Venice, utilised her knowledge of her adopted city to great effect in her highly entertaining series of novels featuring Commissario Guido Brunetti.

Nevertheless, take away the mystery, glitz and the glamour and you'll find that nearly every single piece of writing, fiction or non-fiction, *will* be loosely based on those themes given in the Polti Theory.

⇨ **Rather than waste time trying to buck the system by coming up with original thought – go for an innovative approach.**

People Watching

Nothing we take on board during our daily routine is ever wasted if we are writers, although this doesn't always mean things that happen to us personally, because few of us live life in the fast lane. Quite a large number of those 'happenings' that are of use to us will have involved other people and so we have to learn to become an avid people-watcher – in other words, a snoop! We watch, listen, spy and eavesdrop in order to collect ideas to convert into the written word. Just as we learnt to take notice of everything that happens on our patch, so we extend our awareness to people, what they do, how they react, body language, etc.

Whenever we leave the house and travel to work each day, we have plenty of opportunity for people watching but what happens if we happen to be house-bound, or work from home? In that case we watch life by proxy. All serious writers should take a daily newspaper because this, more often than not, will stimulate the creative processes on a mundane level. Newspaper stories and articles will give you the human angle for any one of the categories given in the Polti Theory, because these are the real-life dramas that sell newspapers. And what better gauge of public interest than the daily scandal-rags or broadsheets?

Listen to conversations going on in public places and jot down what you hear. This is a great source of one-liners, even if the rest of the conversation is missed, or contains nothing of interest. Just as importantly, listen to *how* people say things and express themselves, because this can provide added depth to your character without resorting to long, wordy descriptions. Colloquialisms and similes, especially those of a regional or localised nature can convey volumes if used in the correct context and dispense with the urge to attempt to write in dialect.

➪ **People watching is the writer's fuel for good ideas.**

Body Language & Gestures

What we generally refer to as 'body language' is someone's unconscious reaction to a situation or person. People watching adds a whole new dimension to the way individuals react to one another and, like a picture, can easily convert into 1,000 words of narrative. The married couple who do and say all the right things, and yet their body language may give off conflicting signals at variance with the outward show of domestic bliss. Or the pretty, well-turned out child that does not appear relaxed in the company of a step-parent. Or the dog that refuses to respond to a particular visitor's overtures. Each reaction can be detected in body language.

Gestures also tend to be an unconscious reaction to situations or people, and usually involve making some symbolic movement of the hand. Some are comparatively modern, while others can be traced back hundreds of years, but as Desmond Morris points out in his book, *Gestures*, this is a form of visual slang and just as slang words go out of fashion, so can gestures. Body language and gestures can be used as a 'conflict' device so essential to fiction writing, as a cause of misunderstanding, or the give-away in a thriller.

Secret Step Two enforces the observation that too many people go through life never looking around at what's actually going on in their immediately vicinity. A writer needs to realise the importance of taking the 'time to stand and stare' because this is the only way to add to the inner retrieval system of our cerebral 'zip file'. We must learn to observe in order to be able to record what we see and to be able to retrieve this information when we sit down to write. Because there really is a story, article or poem behind everything we encounter during our daily routine.

⇨ **Accept the fact that writers are, without a doubt, vampiric creatures, in that they can only exist by sucking the life out of any situation or encounter, and it using to further their own writing careers.**

Handy Hint:
People-watching provides us with additional material to use to develop characterisation and the obvious expert on the subject is undoubtedly Desmond Morris. His books, *The Human Zoo, The Naked Ape, Manwatching, Intimate Behaviour* and *Gestures* not only provide hours of entertainment but also plenty of background information about human body language. At least one of these titles should be among a writer's reference collection but they should not be used as substitutes for the real thing, i.e. personal observation. Second hand copies are usually readily available on www.ABE-Books.com

Try This Exercise:
Take a copy of your regular daily national newspaper and mark each of the items that arouse your interest. Cut them out and keep them in files, together with any comments/ideas you might have for future writing projects. As the collection builds you will find that certain subjects occur more and more frequently; others were just a passing whim. Go through this collection every couple of months to stimulate ideas if you're feeling uninspired. Throw away any clippings that no longer interest you. Use this opportunity to jot down ideas for:

- A short story
- An article
- A poem

Chapter Five

Innermost Thoughts

"Writing has laws of perspective, of light and shade, just as painting does or music. If you are born knowing them, fine. If not, learn them. Then rearrange the rules to suit yourself." **Truman Capote**

It was Marcel Proust who said that the voyage of discovery lies not in finding new landscapes, but in having new eyes with which to view them. It was a former tutor of mine, Bob Clay-Egerton, who introduced the concept of the 'mystical mug' into his teachings to demonstrate how we 'see' things:

Pick up an ordinary drinking mug. Imagine that the mug is floating in front of you at eye level, the handle standing out to the left. Imagine now that you are describing exactly what you see to a blind person. *What do you actually see?* Assume you have never seen a mug before; it is a strange and wonderful phenomena. You would have to say you saw a roughly square or rectangular object but perhaps tapering slightly towards the base. It appears to be convex towards you. Standing out to the left is a curved projection, joining the main body just below the top and about two thirds of the way down the body. You describe the colour and decorative pattern if any. Sex? If it has any it must be male, because of the projection.

The blind person then has the mug described to him by someone seeing it from 90 degrees to the right of the first observer. Same general shape, colour, texture and pattern but no projection. It must be similar but not the same. Sex? No projection, so it can't be male. No hollows, so it can't be female. It might, therefore, be neuter. The next description comes from someone viewing the mug directly from above. The basic shape is now circular, either tubular or cylindrical, and flat at the end. A single stem projection juts out from the main body as the top of the handle covers the rest from view. Same colour but no decorative pattern. It cannot be related to the first or second object at all. Sex? Projection indicates male, hollow cylinder indicates female; might be hermaphroditic.

If several people viewing the mug from the top, bottom and four sides (let alone at oblique angles) gave a description, the blind person would assume they were all seeing different objects, some of which may, or may not be related. If each viewer described what he saw to an outsider who had not seen the mug, none of them would believe the others had only described a different view of the same object. Someone familiar with a mug might realise what it was, but even then, the description, if it could be evaluated by those who had never seen one, would not convey what it was made from, how it was constructed, fired, decorated, glazed — or even what its purpose was.

We use for this example of selective angles of viewpoint - a simple mug. Imagine how complicated it would have been to describe, from different angles, an old-fashioned typewriter! The more complex the subject, the harder it is to imagine its nature and purpose. Yet many writers (and some tutors) approach writing from a limited standpoint ... that black is black, and white is white. Never stopping to think that there might be forty shades of grey in between the various different ways a subject might be viewed or written about. There are innumerable planes of existence on different levels, in many dimensions of time and space. Mankind exists, physically, in one dimension ... mentally he can penetrate other levels ... spiritually he can reach even more ... it's all a matter of perspective.

So ... in all aspects of our writing we need to develop the ability to see things from all angles. The successful writer 'sees' everything from every angle and viewpoint, and weighs this in the balance before committing themselves to action. For the purpose of *Life-Writes*, we will substitute our readers for the blind person of the exercise. They can only 'see' from our writing what we want them to see. If our characterisation (in terms of empathy and/or human interest) gives the opposite impression to what we originally intended, then the picture has become distorted and the creative dynamic of the plot or narrative is lost. And if a writer complains that an editor or competition judges has 'missed the point' of a story, then it's probably because it wasn't made clear in the first place.

➯ **Always keep the lesson of the 'mystical mug' in mind!**

Life's like that!

For our next mental exercise we will choose another simple subject that can have many meanings. It would be tempting to go for 'Love' because *Roget's Thesaurus* has something like 33 entries, while the opposite, 'Hate' only has nine! This means we're going to have to work harder and delve deeper.

Firstly, we need to define what we mean by 'hate' because it is a word that is over-used today. We may say we 'hate spiders' but do we really? We may feel frightened, repulsed or nauseated by them – but hate? The dictionary definition of hate is: *"Extreme dislike or aversion; detestation; to abhor or detest; enmity or ill-will; loathing"*, while the on-line Wikipedia has hatred (or hate) as an intense feeling of dislike. "It may occur in a wide variety of contexts, from hatred of inanimate objects or animals, to hatred of oneself or other people, entire groups of people, people in general, existence, or everything."

The depth of expression is largely dependant on the person making the declaration, or the circumstances under which the declaration is made. A trivial person will 'hate' anything and everything that they don't like, from cabbage to an unimaginative wedding present. Someone else may actively hate racial inequality or social injustice, but on the other side of the coin in living memory we have had Holocaust that resulted from Nazi hatred of the Jews. Of the fictional variety, the character of Edmond Dantes in *The Count of Monte Cristo* gives us an epic tale of hatred and revenge. Very few of us would, if we were completely honest, have ever really experienced the true emotion of hatred but there are nine category listed in the Polti Theory that could be fuelled by hatred:

Crime pursued by vengeance
Vengeance taken for kindred upon kindred
Revolt
Enmity of kinsmen
Murderous adultery
Madness
Discovery of the dishonour of a loved one
Mistaken jealousy
Erroneous judgement

Using the same lateral thinking, what, for example, would you consider to be the greatest love story ever written? After careful consideration, *my* choices (and for totally different reasons) would be a toss-up between *Wuthering Heights* and *The Lord of the Rings*. In terms of romantic love, the destructive tide of passion that drives both Catherine and Heathcliffe, renders all other fictional lovers superfluous. The type of love contained within *The Lord of the Rings* is the bond or spark that exists between the 'Fellowship' and is expressed in terms of loyalty and comradeship against over-whelming odds. The actual romantic interlude pales into insignificance beside the heroic deeds of those fighting together against Mordor.

On a purely personal level, both novels can still produce that gut-churning, throat-tightening feeling no matter how many times I read them, and yet neither would qualify as 'love stories' in the traditional sense of the word. When we refer to 'love' in our own writing, we are going to use it in the context of the story-line to give the work 'reader appeal'. We can use it in the bitter, destructive context of the television series, *Mother Love*, which starred Diana Rigg in the title role. Or the desperate variety of *Bridget Jones' Diary*. Or the escapism of *Shirley Valentine*. Love does not necessarily mean 'romance' in Mills & Boon mould and although we might couch it in different terms, it still makes the world go round. Love and hate are highly emotive subjects, so handle with care!

Secret Step Three reveals that no matter how mundane and/or familiar a scene, there are countless different angles from which to view it. Emotions are the very life-blood of creative writing whether we are utilising them in fiction, non-fiction or poetry. Described as 'the various phenomena of the mind' (including anger, joy, fear, sorrow, etc), we also use them to arouse those emotions in our readers – **to make them care about what they read**. Emotions are also extremely complex and we can weave a tangled web of intense feeling within our writing to force our readers to suffer along with our characters, article content or poem.

Neither can emotion (or the reason behind it) be cast in stone. We can be angry – but anger is rarely generated by one single action. It has usually been compounded by numerous smaller, insignificant happenings. We need to create these multi-layers in our writing, especially when creating characters for a novel, because without them the finished piece will lack depth. There was a popular method of encouraging lateral thinking in business management training back in the 1970s called 'mind mapping'. It was an idea-generating technique that breaks down linear thinking – thinking in straight lines – and encourages the mind to work laterally by accessing our 'zip-files' in the right-brain.

Instead of running ideas in a straightforward top-to-bottom list, start by placing the key word in the centre of the page and circle it. As word-association triggers off other ideas, write them down and circle them, linking them to the key word and each other with connecting lines. For this exercise we start with the key-word = fear. As the circles move outwards, we can travel a long way from that original key-word. We may find we've thrown in things that would never have occurred to us when using lists to flesh out a story or article. Mapping is also a useful technique for developing plots and characters and can be included in your Ideas Book when you are stuck for ideas, or don't know where to go next.

⇨ **Whenever you feel the urge to make a list of ideas, use this mapping technique instead. You may find that it can even replace doodling when you're on the telephone.**

Stuck in the Mud

Whenever a group of writers get together, sooner or later the subject of writer's block will be introduced into the equation. In most cases this is an over-milked excuse for not starting or completing a typescript. As I've said before, a professional writer can't afford to employ such a plea for sympathy, although they do recognise the need for regular stimulation to generate ideas.

If an idea isn't working and there isn't a dead-line to meet, the professional will leave it alone and do something else – read a book, do some gardening, take the dog for a walk, or attend to the pile of research material that needs filing. Even the most seasoned writer will 'dry up' from time to time but they don't stop working, they turn their attention to something else for a while.

Dead-lines are probably the most effective means of beating the dreaded blockage since they 'concentrate the mind wonderfully', wrote the late Nancy Smith when she was asked for a comment when I was compiling *From An Editor's Desk. "If a professional writer is commissioned to write a piece by a specific date, it's rare for them not to finish it by then. Writer's block does exist but the main cause is probably due to lack of planning, so far as the novel is concerned, at least. It may be that the story-line isn't strong enough and needs to be abandoned, or it may be that they should leave it for a while, and start on something else until their enthusiasm is re-kindled."*

Many of the techniques discussed in *Life-Writes* are designed to push both our conscious and subconscious minds to extremes, even when we're relaxing. We soon come to realise that some of our best ideas have occurred when we're away from the computer and not thinking about anything remotely connected with writing. An author of my acquaintance recently admitted that she had an astounding flash of creative insight while she was in the middle of cleaning out the cat's litter tray! Hopefully *Life-Writes* will provide more pleasant ways of clearing any blockage because it illustrates that there are more facets to creative writing than sitting at the key board for hours on end, churning out mere words. By taking a break from writing, and under the right conditions/atmosphere/exercises, we can often achieve far more with an hour's relaxation than by forcing ourselves to carry on typing.

Although we need to remain focused on the job in hand, there should be plenty of time allowed for the unconscious mind to put in its own four-penny worth. Thinking side-ways means allowing those right-brain influences to come through even if we happen to be in the middle of writing something else, because those new ideas might make the piece even better.

➪ **Who said you could only have one good idea at a time?**

Handy Hint:
A quick-fix information resource is the Wikipedia on-line encyclopaedia. Log it up as a favourite on your web browser and if you get stuck for a date, name, spelling or reference, it gives instant access. No need to get up from the computer to go rummaging through several books to check out an obscure spelling or Latin name for a plant.

Try This Exercise:
Treat yourself to a writer's research day at your local library and familiarise yourself with *Willings Press Guide,* a comprehensive and up-to-date media guide. Available in three printed volumes, UK, Europe and World (or online) it gives detailed access to the world's media with data on over 71,000 publications and media outlets worldwide, including target audience, and information covering newspapers and magazines in over 200 countries. It lists all the publications you might need in a quick look-up format. Most of us have to rely on the library edition as we can't afford to buy our own.

- Set your goal to find three new potential market outlets on each visit

Chapter Six

Food For Thought

"From time immemorial, the human race has explored the world in search of food ... Empires have done battle for food, civilisations have been built around it, crimes committed, laws made and knowledge exchanged ..." **Maguelonne Toussaint-Samat, *A History of Food***

I have an impressive collection of cookery books – some belonged to my mother and grandmother, others collected by myself over the years. There are regional and foreign cook books; several Mrs Beeton's from the early and mid 1900s; an ancient copy of the French classic *Larousse Gastronomique*; farmhouse cookery and wild food from the hedgerows ... not to mention a dozen of the basic how-to variety including a complete set of the collectable week-by-week magazine, *Supercook*, from the early 1970s.

For a long time now, cookery books have been regularly listed high on the bestseller lists. We have recipes from Victorian kitchens, cottage kitchens, summer picnics, afternoon teas, Christmas feasts, seasonal and regional suggestions, foreign food ... cooking for students and singles, catering on a budget ... in fact, you name it and there's probably a cookery book in print to cater for it. Not to mention the 'how to write about food' guides. And you don't have to have a cordon bleu diploma or be a 'kitchen goddess' to write about food or cookery. There is an extremely large and lucrative market place for the cookery writer and whether you are a blossoming master chef, or simply wanted to share the recipes from your great-grandmother's handwritten notebook, there are lots of opportunities for entering the world of food publishing in the form of books and articles.

The next time you visit any large bookshop, take a look at the number and variety of the cookery books on sale - and make a note of the publishers. Next consider the large number of women's magazines that feature a cookery page and study the depth of detail that goes into each article. But it doesn't stop at the women's magazines ... there is often a seasonal recipe included in *Home Farmer, Farmer's Weekly*, or game recipes in *The Shooting Times*. Any of the field sporting magazines would probably be interested in a simple recipe showing what to do with 'it' once you've caught it! Then there are hundreds of different local recipes for the multitude of regional magazines ...

Without going any further for the moment, we can see the tremendous amount of potential outlets in this field of writing, not to mention restaurant and book reviews. If you can realise the potential and see yourself fitting in to this area of creative writing, invest in a couple of how-to books on the subject and add them to your reference shelf. Unfortunately most of the 'food writing' books listed on Amazon don't include basic how-to advice but the following might help:

Janet Lawrence was cookery correspondent for *The Daily Telegraph* and in *The Craft of Food & Cookery Writing*, she tackles that all-important question of how to identify a winning formula for a cookery book, and explores the possibilities for selling food. Drawing on her experience as an author of numerous cookery books, and an experienced writer of food and cookery articles for many different publications, the guide covers everything the aspiring food and cookery writer needs to know.

The Recipe Writer's Handbook. Barbara Gibbs Ostmann and Janet Baker are experienced food editors who know that writing recipes is a tricky business. To achieve success a recipe must be written with impeccable accuracy and unambiguous clarity and this book offers a wide range of information for both the novice and seasoned cookery writer.

Will Write For Food by Dianne Jacob is a complete guide to cook books, blogs and reviews for anyone wanting to be a food writer. It focuses on the American market rather than the UK but has a lot of sound information for those wishing to branch out in this direction.

Like Faust with his madeleines, food can be extremely evocative - as this extract from a nostalgic article from *The Countryman* shows:

The men have been out in the fields since dawn and will be looking forward to the supper spread out on the kitchen table. Although it's school tomorrow, we have been allowed to stay up late to take part in the feast. No standing on ceremony here. The scrubbed boards provide the only backdrop for the huge ham waiting for carving, with its thick outer layer of white fat and breadcrumbs. It's our father's last job for the day and everyone is quickly served with a generous helping of the succulent, home-cooked meat. Bowls of crisp salad and juicy tomatoes straight from the garden, and buttered new potatoes lifted just that morning, sprinkled with parsley. Hard-boiled eggs from the hen house, and home-made pickles; fresh bread with rich butter and cheese complete the meal …

I can still taste that supper and when I sent a copy of the magazine in which the piece was published to a childhood friend, she immediately remembered those hay-making suppers, which took us both back to being about eight-years old again … *We fidget from the hayseeds and dried grass that have crept under our clothes and into our shoes, but we don't want to move and break the spell…*

Articles don't necessarily have to be about food to be enriched by the subject. I recently read a travel piece that offered some tantalising cameos of the cuisine served aboard a French river cruise ship. There, tucked away in the wealth of detail about people and places were some succulent morsels of the daily fare for the passengers – and resulted in the article being filed away for future reference when a holiday moment occurs! In fact, everywhere we go – both home and abroad – most of us will find a local culinary moment that is worth storing away to share with a readership at some later stage. Such as a wonderful (and colourful) buffet lunch at the Topkapi Palace in Istanbul; or the fabulous fresh sea-food platter served in a restaurant behind the ramparts at St Malo. **Secret Step Four** means that no one can access the same experiences and memories, and that offers you the opportunity to generate unique responses to those situations.

Regional food can also be dove-tailed to provide endless topics for articles, both regionally and nationally, and in a wide variety of publications. Here we can draw on family background, nostalgia, memories (and not necessarily our own), as I did when writing another *Countryman* piece on my partner's memory of cherry picking in the Kent orchards:

> *We break for a hasty lunch of thick salad sandwiches of fresh-picked tomatoes, crisp lettuce and the sharp tang of spring onions, all pulled straight from the garden earlier that morning. There's homemade lemonade and ginger beer for us children, while our mother pours a thick brew of tea from her battered cream thermos flask …*

Bringing it up to date with my own 'four penny worth' … A quick and economical supper that his mother often made from any leftover fruit was a cherry batter served with ice cream or custard. I recently found a similar recipe in a 1930s edition of *The Woman's Treasury for Home & Garden*, discovered at a local car boot sale. *"The cherries were placed in a greased baking dish and sprinkled with caster sugar. They were then covered with batter (the kind used for Yorkshire pudding, but sweetened) and baked in the oven for 40 mins."* Just add the ice cream and step back in time ...

Here are a few more possibilities to consider that could earn a few bob as mini-features, readers' letters or handy kitchen hints:

- Local magazines and newspapers are always interested in the wide range of produce on offer at farmer's markets, particularly when this involves a local family. Include a seasonal recipe featuring an item of produce.

- Recommended mart breakfasts can often find a place in farming publications such as *Farmer's Weekly*. There are some amazing little places tucked away in the corners of some of our traditional market halls. Make sure your 'menu' is mouth-watering, not swimming in grease!

- *Home Farmer* magazine ran a series featuring recipes from around the UK – 'North West Nosebag' included simple ones from the Lake District and Liverpool; while 'Emerald Isle Cuisine' included farm house kitchen ideas not forgetting the Saturday morning must-have – the Irish breakfast or Ulster Fry!

- Simple snacks and inexpensive ideas are always popular – for example: 'Warming Toast Toppers' – but do make sure that you include something for everybody. I get quite excited about new ideas but this enthusiasm quickly evaporates because nearly all the recipes contain cheese and I have a serious cheese allergy.

- Growing food with no garden – you would be surprised exactly how much food you can produce on an average-sized patio and these ideas could earn prizes from the readers' letters pages in a wide variety of publications.

> Economy hint: use the cardboard of toilet rolls inside plastic ice cream cartons for planting seeds instead of buying mini peat pots.

And what about those wonderful 1950s home-from-school treats of cheese and potato pie made with butter and half a pint of cream (or full milk); bubble and squeak (or bubble and squelch as its called in some areas) and 'eggy bread'. The ideas might give the food police heart failure but on a cold winter's day an editor might just think it's a tastier alternative to beans on toast.

Old fashioned remedies and household hints are also popular but these need to have an unusual or unexpected spin to bring them up to date. For example, it's a well-known fact that onions are a magnet for bacteria and that they've been used in sick rooms to 'draw' the germs for generations. We've known of cut onions being used in racing kennels to prevent kennel sickness. This was normal operating procedure in 150-dog kennel when there was sickness about and none of the greyhounds ever came down with it.

⇨ **For the writer, *everything* is food for thought.**

Character Building

It's been said that 'we are what we eat', and food can also play an important part in fiction writing as a device to give insight into a character's background and personality. How and what we eat can speak volumes about a person and their lifestyle. If we wish to convey wealth then our characters will consume copious amount of champagne; poverty can be summed up with bread and dripping. Lavish banquets can set the scene in historical fiction, while wartime rationing gives a sense of camaraderie in coupon sharing. Food fads are also a sign of the times and our characters will need to reflect what is 'in' and what is 'out', especially if the fiction is a period piece.

Consider that every part of the world has its own instantly recognisable style of preparing and offering food, and can help set the scene for readers; to jog memories and draw them into your story. How many of these scenes can you 'see' just from a brief mention of the food?

- Freshly baked bagels from a Jewish Sunday morning bakery;
- Traditional fish 'n chips in an English seaside resort;
- Christmas cake baking in grandma's kitchen;
- A trucker's breakfast from an old fashioned 'greasy spoon';
- Roast lamb in a Greek taverna;
- The distinctive aroma of a Parisian street café;
- The spice market in Istanbul;
- Toffee apples from a visiting fair;

To make them come alive, our characters need these evocative settings and what better device than using food as a backdrop. But don't do as one budding novelist did. Her male lead was a bit of a 'foodie' and whenever he and the heroine got together there was a complete menu offered up at every encounter, complete with a vintage wine! By chapter six I was feeling distinctly queasy and by the end of the book both characters would have weighed in at least 20 stone! Not 'over-egging the pudding' is a culinary hint worth remembering in fiction writing.

When writing period pieces, it's also worth studying books of etiquette for the period, which can provide hours of entertainment and offer all sorts of ideas for domestic incidents that will make the characters more convincing. The newly-wed wife who entertains her in-laws for the first time; a young man's first formal ball; covering up a servant's mistake; the ordeal of the ballroom. There are still old books on etiquette to be found through second-hand booksellers that give advice on such matters. Such as:

The Book of Etiquette by Lady Troubridge. First published in 1926 and remained in print until the 6th impression in 1976.

Etiquette for Gentlemen and *Etiquette for Ladies* from Ward Lock. Not dated so probably a much earlier version than the above. *The Gentlemen* warns that 'a man may forgive you for breaking his daughter's heart, but never for breaking his hunter's neck!'

Etiquette by Emily Post (1922) for the American version of acceptable manners, which vary slightly from the English and often more draconian.

The books also contain valuable information on what to serve and when … 'Second helpings are not offered at dinner-parties' … as well as suggested menus for afternoon tea, informal luncheons, batchelor dinners, etc., and more importantly how to eat them.

Food can add splashes of colour to a story. Did you know, for example that although bread, ale, meat and fish were the staple diet of medieval England, fish often came from as far away as Iceland, and as early as 1480 over 100,000 oranges were being imported? Where did this snippet come from? *Food & Feast in Medieval England* by Peter Hammond, who is author on several academic books of the period. Imagine a romantic interlude whereby the heroine tastes her first orange; or meets the stranger who accompanies the Icelandic catch …

Another Sutton title, *Memory, Wisdom & Healing: The History of Domestic Plant Medicine* by Gabrielle Hatfield, chronicles the historic use of plants by ordinary people for coughs and colds, cuts and bruises, burns and other everyday ills. The author is an Honorary Research Associate at the Royal Botanic Gardens whose research on domestic plant remedies won her the Michaelis-Jena Ratcliff Prize for Folklore. Imagine how this sort of information on domestic plant medicine could enrich a story – past or present.

Similarly, Dutch Egyptologist Lise Manniche gives us *An Ancient Egyptian Herbal* and *Sacred Luxuries: Fragrance, Aromatherapy and Cosmetics in Ancient Egypt*. The first title includes the use of plants in the garden, home and kitchen, as well as those used in medicine; the second focuses on the importance of perfumes and cosmetics. Imagine your ancient Egyptian heroine experimenting with a new cosmetic … in just the same way as a 2012 teenager trying out a new Boots' eye shadow.

While kicking all these ideas around in our head, let's think for a moment about the run-away foodie success of Joanne Harris's novel, *Chocolat*, that reflected the not so subtle conflict between the 'solemnity of the church' in provincial France, and a pagan hedonistic delight of chocolate. A whole novel woven around the wicked little cocoa bean!

➪ **A writer's characters can't live by bread alone!**

Handy Hint:
Don't be afraid of using academic books for source material. You'll often come across information not generally available to add zest to your story. You'll also find that academics are more generous with their time and less precious about their copyright than commercial authors. If you require further information or clarification of a particular point, an emeritus professor of history will generally be more than happy to provide the material you require.

Try This Exercise:

In Chapter One we casually mentioned the idea of creating a 'sports luncheon' for the ladies while the men are glued to the television, participating in, or off watching the event. Try creating an article or short story featuring a lunch to coincide with a major sporting event – Ryder Cup (golf); Cheltenham Gold Cup (racing); Grand Prix (motor racing); Test Match (cricket); Cup Final (football); Twickenham (rugby) – that you might offer to a women's magazine or a sporting publication.

Chapter Seven

Lost in Thought

Reverie: [French rêverie, to dream.] Listless musing; a day-dream; a loose or irregular train of thought; a wild or fantastic vision.
The Waverley Modern English Dictionary

Let's go back to the famous adage of writing about what you know. Nearly everything we write is, in some way, autobiographical. That is, we draw on our own life experiences and turn them into fact or fiction. Think about it. Everyday we tell somebody a 'story' about something that has happened to ourselves, or a friend, the dog, or a member of the family. We re-create the scene for dramatic effect, to make people laugh, gain sympathy, etc., while minimising or maximising our own personal involvement in the story. We do this for several reasons:

- we want to give a particular slant to the story
- the story needs livening up
- the story shows us in a favourable light
- the story doesn't show us in a particularly favourable light
- we need to abdicate any responsibility for what happened
- we feel the need to appear more important
- we need to shift the blame

The older we are, the more experience and resources we have to draw on for story-telling. Although the media makes a great fuss of any bright, new talent that comes along, those who've passed the Big 4-0 have written a larger number of first novels. Of course, it pays to follow the general guideline of writing about what we know but the older we get the more opportunities we have had for observing the behaviour and life-styles of those different to ourselves over a wider passage of time. Even if we are only involved on the periphery of another way of life, the viewpoint of the uninformed observer can also be used to enhance a story-line.

Which, of course, brings us back to the subject of writing about what we know. Here again, we must look at perspective and viewpoint and, if we want to be pedantic, define the meaning of the word 'know' in writer's jargon. Most writing tutorials insist on us sticking to what we 'know' and yes, it does give an aura of credibility to the text, but does this mean we can never step outside the world of which we have first-hand experience?

Let's look at Janice ... and Rosie

Janice has had over twenty year's nursing experience, specialising in midwifery, but she doesn't want to restrict her writing to hospital romances and articles for nursing journals – she wants to be a science fiction writer. She's lost count of the times she's been told that she should 'stick to what she knows' and write about nursing, even though she's fed up with it. What does she do?

Firstly: Janice already has had a couple of articles published in the professional journals and has now been encouraged to try a slightly different angle with some of the weekly women's magazines. Even though she's lost interest in nursing as a full-time career, it can still provide her with that necessary 'shot in the arm' that all writers get from seeing their work in print while she works on her fiction. A modest portfolio of non-fiction successes will support the proposal for her novel when she sends it out, because she will be viewed in a more sympathetic light than an absolute beginner. She wouldn't be the first freelance writer to subsidise novel writing from a successful career in non-fiction.

Secondly: After a rather intense brain-storming session at her local writers' group, she came up with the core idea of a medical crew aboard a spaceship being sent to investigate why all the new-born babies of the inter-galactic colonists were mysteriously dying. Since human biology was unlikely to alter much in the sf-future, her personal experience added weight to the reality of the explanations to non-medical characters and the dialogue between the medical team. Once she had gotten over her antipathy towards the inclusion of medicine in the plot, she became really enthusiastic about the idea.

Science fiction writer Rose Oliver, however, highlights the difficulties involved in writing about an unfamiliar world. *"I think, for example, that science fiction writing demands more creativity than other genres because while other writers can draw on the past and present for background, plots etc., sf writers have nothing like this to grab hold of from the future. In my story, 'Cold Pressure', published in* Jupiter *magazine the underwater scene was a humdinger to pull together. My protagonists were in a cave's air pocket. What would they see? Oops! No light. Enter stage right, phosphorescent plankton. The protagonists needed oxygen. Now where would that come from? Then I discovered some seaweed had oxygen-filled bladders. O.K. Let's make them bigger and popping. Even better, their popping movement would make the plankton light up and grow. The seaweed would then feed off the dead plankton. Yippee! Got a mini-world. Next came drinking water. In a sea? Impossible. Give up on story. A while later, husband mentioned fresh water could be pressed out of fish. Back to story..."*

Obviously Rosie Oliver isn't writing about a world she knows, and even her characters have to be moulded by the science and society of their time. *"In the novel I am rewriting, the heroine has been born and brought up under a much higher gravity than those she lives and works with. She has to be more careful not to break things, forcing her to act in a more deliberate manner. It makes her more precise in both thought and action. This, in turn, means she survives dangerous situations with split second judgement when her colleagues cannot. When we first meet her, she has already left a trail of dead partners who did 'not make the grade'. And as for the bedroom... She is nicknamed 'The Ice' for very good reasons. Putting such an unusual rounded character together from a background detail takes quite a bit of time and brainwork!"*

Imagine the extra work necessary to evolve a plot from an innovative premise; build the background world from scratch; and align characters with their unusual world. But as we can see, writing about what we know doesn't necessarily mean placing restrictions on what we can write about. It means utilising personal knowledge, background, interests and experience and moving it into another dimension, if necessary. As with life in general, we have to understand why the rules are there and what purpose they serve before we set our story in ancient Egypt, feudal Japan or the distant future.

Creative energy fuels creativity, so immerse yourself with creative images and stimulating art forms to give fresh ideas and ignite the creative flame. **Secret Step Five** is tapping into whatever can unleash creative energy.

➯ **But where do those ideas come from?**

Roots & Memories

Most of us would say that we come from very ordinary backgrounds. That is, before we start reminiscing and going over the family history and realise that there's an awful lot of material there from which to draw. This doesn't mean sitting down and writing a family saga, but it does offer the opportunity to scatter little cameos throughout our writing based on factual or anecdotal family stories. It also encourages us to follow the tangled skeins and discover new information about our own heritage. Look how popular the television series, *Who Do You Think You Are?* has become – and what remarkable stories have been revealed about very ordinary people.

For example: when leafing through *A Dictionary of English Surnames,* I came across the entry for *'Slaymaker div. A weaver's reed or shuttle. Always a rare name. Formerly more common but now apparently extinct'*. Now Slaymaker was my maternal great-grandmother's maiden name and our relations still lived on the family farm in the village until the late 1970s when the elder son died in a farming accident and the younger son moved away after the father hung himself in the barn. There's got to be a 'cameo' in there somewhere ... along with the grandfather who was awarded the Scouting's Medal of Merit by Lord Baden Powell ... a great aunt who claimed to have been a music-hall entertainer although we all suspected her occupation was something far less respectable! ... another great aunt who served as a nurse with Edith Cavell. My maternal grandmother was head cook at a Derbyshire country estate that played host to the then Prince of Wales for a shooting party; she could remember talk about the sinking of the Titanic, and below-stairs gossip of the time that linked the Duke of Clarence with Jack the Ripper long before popular television raised the question.

Most families have a 'sheep fold' where all the black sheep have been consigned over the years – and very few of us come from pure Celtic or Anglo-Saxon stock. There's all sorts of mixes in our blood-lines that account for family feuds that go on for generations. Even if we are an 'only child', in our immediate family we have four different strains from each of our grandparents. And what about all those 'uncles and aunts' that hover about on the periphery, who are no relation at all and yet have always been considered part of the extended family. My father had one such 'Uncle Jack' who'd been a military doctor during the Zulu wars and who had brought home a shield and assegai from Rourke's Drift, having arrived at the site after the battle to treat the wounded. Then there are the internecine squabbles that drive families apart through lies and deceit – not to mention the tales of missing jewellery after the funeral, and the Birthday Book!

Never under estimate your family connections, dead or alive they can provide rich pickings for many years to come, so long as you treat each one like a little gem and not squander them wantonly. As Jeff Heffron writes in *The Writer's Idea Book: "Use heritage – ethnic and familial – as material for your writing. It's probably the richest source you possess."* And remember, you don't have to cast them in their own period; you can move them around in time and space, wherever you choose.

Our roots, or family background, often give a personal insight into why we behave towards certain people in a particular manner. Did someone, or something, have a control or influence over us that was either rewarding, or detrimental to our development? My mother could remember living in fear of getting a clout across the back of the legs from her grandmother's walking stick, which the old girl used to administer when neither of her parents were looking. She never dared tell them because it wasn't the done thing to report such matters.

It's not just family who can provide us with background information and character-cameos for our writing. Every place we visit, every passing stranger is grist for our respective writing mill as we observe, catalogue and file away snippets of 'life' to be recycled and examined as and when the need arises. What about the old chap whom you wave to every morning as he sits by his window day after day? You haven't a clue who he is, or why he sits there, but there's a short story, article and poem in there if you think about it hard enough.

⇨ **As we sit in cafes, or wander around the museum, there are dozens of 'invisible' people all with a story to tell.**

Personal Psychology

Knowing how to express ourselves means that we can also analyse why those things that have lost their power, had any 'power' over us in the beginning. For example:

- Encountering a loathed former teacher
- An ex-mother in law
- A song that belongs to an acrimonious parting or love affair
- Family obligation
- The school or office bully

Any of the above may have caused us a considerable amount of grief and upset at some time in the past. The former teacher, mother in law, or bully encountered many years later will probably bring us face to face with the realisation that they no longer have any 'power' over us because we have out grown their sphere of influence, either in stature or position. Inwardly we would probably express surprise that this 'power' has stayed with us for so long but in truth it was only ever effective when we were young, gauche and inexperienced. Now the tables have turned, it is we who are in a position of 'power' because they no longer intimidate us.

"Extraordinary how potent cheap music is," says Amanda in the original script for *Private Lives,* reflecting on the emotive responses caused by a popular song. For years afterwards the unexpected playing of a particular song has the power to resurrect all manner of conflicting emotions that we'd considered dead and buried. Then, for no reason at all, or because of a change in our circumstances, the song suddenly loses its power – and we're finally free of it sneaking up on us when we least expect it. I used this technique in my novel, *The Wild Horseman,* where the traditional song, *Bonnie Dundee,* was the hero's signature tune.

Obligations to an extended family often result from a desire not to offend an elderly relation for whom we have a great deal of respect and affection. Once the elderly relative dies, we are free of any family obligation to cousins, aunts and uncles whom we've never much cared for anyway. The 'power' was exercised by our fondness for the elderly relative, not the family itself, and once those bonds have been severed, it is an ideal opportunity to unload the psychic vampire of misplaced obligation.

⇨ **Record your ideas for things that have lost their power with the passing years.**

Thought & Form

We have to accept that whatever we write about often reflects our own personal philosophy, beliefs or morality. Because we feel strongly about something means that we can inject extra passion into dialogue and it can be a useful device in fiction to have one of your characters expound these ideas; conversely, in non-fiction it can bog down the text and turn it into the dreaded 'opinion piece'. However we intend to use this device, it is essential that the narrative does not descend into megalomania either on the part of our characters, or on us as the writer. Fictional characters can engage in polemic dialogue/discussion in order to make a point or set a scene, but confrontational non-fiction is generally only acceptable to an editor when submitted by celebrity writers.

Outré social or political statements need to be riveting and convincing because a publisher or editor will rarely take a risk on a new writer dabbling in this field, unless there is some authentic background to support the research – whether fiction or non-fiction. A device I used in my novel, *Whittlewood,* was to allow one of the characters to make certain pertinent social statements by way of an interview that was being conducted as part of the story-line. This gave room for manoeuvre when the journalist queried or wanted to clarify a point.

To see how people put an opinion across in an interview, study how the points are made in those published in the weekend colour supplements to the broadsheets. The interviewer not only reports on responses to pertinent questions, but also comments on appearance, manner and body language to complete the picture. This is one of the best methods of painting pictures by people using economy of language, especially if trying to make a social or political statement without getting bogged down with description and narrative. A good journalist can convey these images in thumb-nail sketches, while not missing out on the essential point of the interview – a trick that most fiction writers would benefit from studying.

Many ideas begin life as personal memories and, although they are important to us as the individuals who have experienced them, unless we have already attained celebrity status, our personal memories and reflections are of little interest to others – particularly editors and publishers. The original idea might have its roots in fact but it may be more marketable to develop it into the form of a short story, or a poem, which can often provide a new dimension to what started out as a straight forward, real-life experience.

Already, the contents of our Ideas Book should be growing at a rapid rate as we discover new ways of expressing ideas, viewpoints and sentiments. This is why, unlike many writing tutorials, I ask you not to use my ideas but to substitute your own for the different categories of 'things' and exercises. I have been drawing on what I know (from experience, background, family, personal interest, reading, researching) and, to be a successful writer, you need to draw on what *you* know, whether on a conscious or subconscious level.

As we've already seen, writing about what we know, doesn't mean restricting our subject matter. To 'know', according to the dictionary is: *"To have a clear and certain perception of; to recognise from memory or description, to identify; to be convinced of the truth or reality of; to be acquainted with; to have personal experience of; to be familiar with; to be on intimate terms with; to be aware of; to understand from learning or study."* Which means we can also write about those things we care to acquire knowledge about in order to extend our personal viewpoint or perspective for the purpose of scene-setting.

⇨ **Make a list of all the things you'd like to know more about in your Ideas Book – and start reading.**

Handy Hint:
Always keep an eye open for reference books, particularly dictionaries, in charity shops, car boot and yard sales - especially any relating to your own developing fields of interest. These can be obtained at a fraction of the original cost and hasn't made a dent in your pocket if you discard them at a later date.

Try This Exercise:
Think of several subjects that you would like to know more about and, using the mind mapping technique described earlier, explore areas of how you can use each of them in your own writing. For example, using Japan as the key-word, we might come up with a poem, article or short story based on a visiting Japanese exhibition. Or a kabuki performance. Or a season of Kurosawa films at the National Film Theatre. Or an object found at a car boot sale. Or watching a Japanese tourist on a visit London. Some degree of study or learning about Japan is, of course, necessary but it doesn't mean that the piece needs to have an in-depth Japanese setting for us to be able to write about it.

- What subject would you choose?

Chapter Eight

Ordeal By Fire

"It's been said that divination was as commonplace in the past as satellite communication is today: it was part of everyday life."
Melusine Draco, *MEAN STREETS WITCHCRAFT*

MB&S or 'mind body and spirit' is one of the fastest growing interests in contemporary publishing. Although many people can be forgiven for thinking that the genre relates to weird folk doing something strange in the woods, the subject matter is now open to readers (and writers) from all walks of life. In the early days of 'alternative belief' publications back in the 1970s, the majority of magazines were home-produced, small press affairs and often difficult to locate. Since the advent of the Internet, all that has changed, and there is now a general sharing of spiritual and 'green' ideas that do not compromise anyone's religious or spiritual integrity.

For those with northern European roots – particularly Celtic, Scandinavian and Germanic – there has always been a love of ghost stories, the supernatural, folklore and a strong tradition in fairies, or the 'little people'. The attraction has persisted down the ages, and even the vampire is alive and well, and living in various prime-time television series. This element of writing has come a long way since the introduction of the 19th century Gothic *Fantasmagoria* or *Tales of the Dead,* which inspired Mary Shelley and John Polidori to write *Frankenstein* and *The Vampyre*. According to Dr Terry Hale, the popularity of these tales of terror was also closely linked to the 'emergence of a new literary genre that frequently employed traditional folk-motifs coupled with increasingly sophisticated narrative techniques.'

Today, on the supermarket and newsagents' shelves we find glossy monthly magazines such as *Prediction, Spirit & Destiny, High Spirits*, etc., that are aimed at the readers' developing interested in holistic health, emotional well-being and spiritual guidance. Various forms of divination, from astrology to zoanthropy, also feature widely in each issue. The following are examples of the subject matter found in some recent MB&S magazines, which differ very little from articles regularly featured in mainstream women's glossies – only the writing style/approach is slightly different by being tailored to suit the 'alternative' readership.

Holistic health:

- How to give up addiction
- Bio-energy healing therapy
- Holistic approach to varicose veins
- Ten tips to stop smoking
- Cleansing foods to spring-clean the body and soul
- The health benefits of eating tofu
- Natural beauty
- Soul food

Emotional well-being:

- Tantra, love and sexuality
- Crystals for attracting love into your life
- Toxic relationships
- Love and the limbic brain
- Past life support
- Retail therapy
- Films as a counselling aid
- Celebrate the Equinox/Solstice

Spiritual guidance:

- Fate – things happen for a reason

- My son's bedroom is a spirit portal
- Life after death
- Bless this house
- What you didn't know about fairies
- Freaky Friday 13th
- Who's your inner goddess?
- Revealed at a séance

Divination:

- Numerology
- Horoscopes/Astrology
- Astro yoga
- Teach yourself Tarot
- I-Ching
- Psychic phone lines
- The dream doctor
- Crystal oracles
- Dowsing

The difference in approach when writing for MB&S magazines and mainstream women's magazines is the use of appropriate jargon, and we need to be familiar with this in order to produce publishable material. We must also convey the impression that we actually believe in, and have practical experience in the subject we are writing about. And if you're still not convinced, don't forget that anything connected with Prince Charles's interest in alternative health treatment is newsworthy, despite the fact that he is constantly criticised for supporting holistic techniques. There is also a rumour that his daughter-in-law Kate is a kindred spirit, and may become patron of a new charity offering alternative therapies.

There are also the glossy pagan magazines such as *Kindred Spirit, Pentacle* and *Pagan Dawn* (the journal of the Pagan Federation) that are available by subscription only. The content of these particular publications covers the same topics as the MB&S magazines, but the emphasis is more on things magical, earth mysteries and the emergence of Wicca as a recognised spiritual belief. This is a much more specialist market and anyone submitting material would need to have more than a passing interest. Generally speaking the pagan publications are non-paying.

Many of the more general aspects of MB&S writing – particularly green issues - are now finding their way into the more orthodox religious magazines. And if we have an interest in issues that are compatible, we can also consider submitting material to the Protestant, Catholic and Jewish publications. Whichever market we are aiming at, we must avoid the polemic or controversial, and maintain a well-balanced and respectful approach to the beliefs of others ... even if they are not our own.

⇨ **Any insincerity or tongue in cheek approach will be instantly rejected.**

The Sacred and the Profane

It is often difficult to express what we personally consider to be sacred things, simply because this concept can vary enormously from person to person. According to the dictionary, sacred means: *Dedicated to religious use, consecrated, dedicated or dear to a divinity; set apart, reserved, or specially appropriated to; pertaining to or hallowed by religion or religious service, holy; sanctified by religion, reverence, etc. not to be profaned,* but does this mean that an atheist or non-religious person can hold nothing sacred? Taking it in its abstract form, if a 'thing' is considered sacred by one religion, it must follow that *all* religious 'things', regardless of the divinity to whom they are dedicated, must also be held to be sacred.

For example, in *Creative Pathways,* I listed the following as being sacred to me personally – regardless of creed or culture:

- Ancient places of worship
- Graveyards and burial sites
- Religious icons
- Holy texts
- Nature

Profanity, on the other hand, is very much a man-imposed condition. One of the best examples of what is usually meant by 'sacred and profane' are the closing sequences in Walt Disney's *Fantasia*, which uses music and imagery to compare *Night on Bald Mountain* with a rather sugary version of *Ave Maria*. The implication is that profanity is the opposite of sacred and therefore, by qualification, must be devil-inspired or evil. In esoteric circles, however, there is an old saying: *"Show me a profane site and I'll show you a fool!"* Meaning that a site, place or object can never be held to be evil – only defiled or desecrated by human agency. Again the dictionary confirms profanity to be a human condition: *Not initiated into sacred or esoteric rites or knowledge; irreverent towards holy things; impious, blasphemous; heathenish; common; vulgar. To treat with irreverence; to desecrate, to violate, to pollute.*

When writing for the MB&S market it is essential to keep this perspective in mind. And if you are unfamiliar with this marketplace, try this simple exercise:

- What would you consider to be profanity against something held by some to be sacred?

- Is there a story or poem in there?

Although the MB&S magazine market is rapidly expanding, it is in the area of book publishing that the genre has taken gigantic strides. Turn to any mainstream publisher's catalogue and we will find a wide selection of subjects within the mind, body and spirit categories:

> Shamanism : Self-Help and Awareness : Meditation : Personal Growth : Qabalah : Paganism : Druidism : Mysticism : Self-esteem and Success : Sexuality : Tantra : Stress Management : Women's Interest : Holistic Health : Astrology : I-Ching : Environment : Earth Mysteries : Channelling : Feng Shui : Paranormal : Mediumship : Wicca : Reincarnation : Reiki : Spirit Guides : Crystals : Plant Medicine : Tarot : Magic : Aromatherapy ...

Needless to say, these are not subjects for the lay-person, but those with a serious interest and practical experience can produce a reader-friendly guidebook. My first foray into the self-help MB&S genre was a co-authored venture with *Exploring Spirituality.* The book only reached modest sales figures but it was a useful insight into the way how-to and self-help books need to be presented - and it did result in my being published in India when the subsidiary rights were sold! It is very often the way a writer presents a subject, rather than the depth of the subject matter, that grabs the publisher's interest.

In this instance, there were dozens of books on personal spirituality but we approached the subject from the viewpoint of those who had become disenchanted with their own religion, and wished to explore other spiritual paths. Using examples and quotes from people from different faiths we were able to offer a wide debate on what people expected from their family religion ... and where they felt they'd been let down. To provide the balance, we invited a member of the 'clergy' from that particular faith to give a response. Needless to say, books of this nature required some form of conclusion or summing-up: we found that those who were dissatisfied or critical of the family faith, were those who were resentful of the refusal to bend the 'rules' to suit their own personal circumstances, rather than any dissatisfaction with the faith as a whole.

Although we are talking about a serious non-fiction book,

there still needs to be an element of tension and drama, not to mention humour – and we always need to keep a couple of surprises until the end. If the reason for writing any non-fiction book is to impart the details of original thought/method/technique, then the reader needs to be led towards this as a satisfactory conclusion. We do not divulge this new information at the beginning – like a good novel, we need to keep the momentum going with history and anecdote until we are ready to spring our surprise.

With *Exploring Spirituality*, our conclusion showed at even in these enlightened times of free speech and political correctness, many of the people questioned believed they had the right to flout the rules without censorship, and yet still remain part of a formal religious grouping. The reason behind the antagonism was the refusal of the 'clergy' to condone their behaviour, but which went against the teaching of that particular religious establishment. These are, of course, tricks of the trade but I personally feel that non-fiction requires just as much creativity as fiction writing.

➪ **Your closing lines must have all the impact of your opening lines.**

The Creative Spirit

Since we are discussing the MB&S genre, let's look at some alternative thoughts on how to stimulate our creative processes. Creativity has been described as an inner state of being and, as Vivienne Crowley pointed out in *Free Your Creative Spirit*: *"It is fed by sensory experience – sight, sound, smell, taste and touch – as processed by our brains and stored in our memories. Our imagination harnesses these sensory impressions to create something that is greater than the sum of the parts – a new creative idea."* More often than not these 'sensory experiences' happen naturally to trigger creative thought.

On other occasions we need to create them for ourselves by paying attention to the atmosphere in which we work; or by introducing certain relaxation elements into our lives. There has always been mirth directed at those who have a special 'writing' sweater (or similar garment) that they put on when they sit down at the keyboard but this isn't as daft as it first appears. This is a person's way of telling the subconscious that the brain should now switch over into 'writing time'. And by developing this particular thought process successfully, the two personalities (the writer and the everyday-person) are balanced and complete in themselves, and do not spill over into each other.

We can, of course, use MB&S techniques to help improve our writing because **Secret Step Six** means drawing creative energy from other sources; such as encouraging the flow of creative energy from our unconscious mind through visualisation, meditation and relaxation techniques.

Atmosphere

Some writers surround themselves with all sorts of weird and wonderful stuff when they sit down to write and the only advice that can be given is: *if it's right for you, do it!* Some like a completely clear work surface; other need to be surrounded by crystals and pictures; shelves of books close by stimulate the creative juices of many more. There are those who like to sit by a window – while others prefer to face a bare wall. It's all a matter of personal preference but wherever we write, it should be somewhere where we feel comfortable and relaxed: the 'right' atmosphere is the one that feels comfortable for the individual.

A working atmosphere can be enhanced by music or silence; a radio playing in another room helps disguise intrusive sounds from outside. Some writers are exponents of café-writing where they can shut out the sights and sounds of fellow customers. One writer completed a whole novel in less than six months while commuting to and from London on a daily basis. We live in an age of the laptop, so in theory, we can write anywhere and at any time we choose. Your friend may work with a thundering great crystal perched on the top of her computer and surrounded by billowing clouds of camphor vapour (for stimulating intuition), but if all you can think of is moth-balls, then don't bother with it. Everyone's relaxation methods are different so if, despite all the suggestions, you throw them all out of the window and stick with a little light Mozart, then that is what's right for you.

Relaxation

If our writing time is governed by family commitments and/or a career, then it is even more important to come to it in a reasonably relaxed frame of mind because this time is precious. Most writing tutorials say that it is necessary to write something everyday but it's not always possible to find the time, or the energy. Perhaps we need to be able to induce a creative atmosphere - with the use of light, sound, perfume and/or some simple relaxation techniques if necessary. Here we are creating a natural firebreak between everyday life and our writing time. If we clear some space between the daily routine and our creative time, it makes it more difficult for diversions to cross over into our 'writing space'. Needless to say, we can't expect to learn how to relax in one easy lesson. If life were that simple, no one would suffer from stress or anxiety, and so we begin by teaching ourselves – not how to 'switch-off' – but how to 'tune-in'.

Firstly, stimulate your appreciation of smell by experimenting with different essential oils – either added to your bath water or in an oil evaporator – or perfumed candles. Most people now accept that some of these oils can produce psychological and/or emotional responses. Combined with a perfumed atmosphere, candlelight produces its own dreamy, quality-time. Mood music can also help to create a state of calm and well-being, especially those recordings harmonising music with natural sounds of bird-song and falling water – unless it makes you want to keep going to the lavatory. Avoid vocal music (with the exception of Gregorian chanting) as lyrics can intrude on your reverie and form a distraction, especially if it's Leonard Cohen or Bob Dylan! If you can't get the sitting-room or bedroom to yourself, retreat to the bathroom and run yourself a deep, scented bath.

Learn how to be 'busy doing nothing' because quality think time is just as important as sitting at the computer, staring at the screen for hours on end. Like all things that take a long time when we're first starting out, you'll find it quicker and easier to slip into relaxed-enough-for-writing mode, the more accomplished you get. Eventually, you should get to the stage where you only need to light a perfumed candle on your desk and you'll be able to tune-in automatically – almost like autosuggestion, but it's you who's calling the tune.

Here are a few simple techniques that can help you relax:
This simple exercise is a friend's method of 'earthing' after a yoga sequence, but it can be used at anytime during the day when there is 10 minutes to spare. It is best performed lying flat on the floor, legs slightly apart and feet flopped to the sides. Arms should be to the side, with hands relaxed, so that you can visualise your body sinking slowly into the ground. Eyes can be open or closed. We are not attempting to push any thoughts away, but allowing them to float across the mind like a TV screen with the sound turned off. There is no need to concentrate on holding any particular mental image – just let things drift. When you feel calm, gently raise your hands above your head and sit up slowly. Now you are ready to begin writing.

Lucid dreaming is a half-waking, half-dream state where we remain fully conscious and aware of our surroundings but still able to receive images or impressions. The image is often superimposed over the immediate surroundings like a double-exposure on a photograph. The best results are obtained by staring at a candle flame in a patch of sunlight, where we need to concentrate on the flickering flame to prevent it from becoming invisible in the sunshine. A good technique for generating ideas.

The term meditation often produces the wrong set of images, especially if viewed in connection with freeing inner thought and creativity. Here we are looking at the discipline as a means of focusing our attention, alleviating stress, or as another of those firebreaks between a daily working routine and creative-time. It is important to understand that here we are also using meditation purely as a 'tool' - as a practical exercise - and should not credit it with any mystical over/undertones. Meditative practices of all kinds reduce stress, help us relax, and encourage sustained concentration.

It is, therefore, possible to utilise meditation on a purely practical level without compromising any personal integrity - simply because there has been a concentrated effort to demystify the practice as therapeutic researchers become more and more aware of the beneficial effects. Different schools of thought favour particular techniques but there is a common denominator – a focal point of attention to which the mind can return when distracted It can also be sitting quietly in an armchair, stroking the cat or doing some sort of needlework, while your subconscious mind 'takes five'.

Alternatively, find somewhere where you can sit undisturbed for at least 15 minutes at a stretch. The best position is one of complete repose and, having assumed a comfortable position, you must try to let the whole body relax. All the muscles must be loosened; all tension let go. The next step is to empty the mind of everything except the problem … breathe in and out, and count one in your head. Repeat, and count two, and so on up to ten. Then begin at one again. After three cycles of counting to ten, stop counting and simply focus on the sensations and movements each breath brings. This may be the rise and fall of your chest; the intake of exhalation in your nostrils; the 'feel' of the air; or any other sensations. Although it takes some practice, it should be possible to be able to banish all thoughts from your mind except the awareness of the physical sensation of breathing. When your 5-10 minutes is up, allow the mind to come back to the 'problem' and you may find it has been resolved by unconsciously tapping into the right-brain.

Do you remember the story of Proust's madeleines in *Remembrance of Things Past?* Where the hero's childhood is evoked by the sensory act of dunking the small, French breakfast cake into his coffee? The visualisation was so intense that he really believed that he had turned the clock back. Most of us find that we can be transported elsewhere by certain smells and that this involuntary transition produces in us the most amazing, almost physical sensations for the few seconds it lasts. The dictionary definition of visualisation is: *To make visual or visible; to make visible to the eye; to externalise or give visible form to an idea, mental image, etc.* By using visualisation techniques, we can run ideas through our mind in picture form to such a degree that they almost become real. We can work through a scene, or dialogue between two characters and see how things work out – sometimes the characters take over and play the scene differently to the one we wanted to write. Sit quietly in a relaxed atmosphere and conjure up the mental image of any one of them – or an image of your own choosing.

Visualisation enables us to project an image or happening onto the wide-angled screen of our mind and play it over and over again – or completely rewrite the script. As with a lot of things, practice does make perfect and it is a proven technique for overcoming problems with characters or plots that have become bogged down. I use this method for injecting fresh (re)actions into supporting players, because all too often we concentrate on the main players and have nothing left for the rest of the cast to do, or say. It's an ideal way of trying out two, or even three, different viewpoints in order to come up with the most effective idea.

At the end of the day, you still need to produce a marketable piece of writing, so there is little point in producing pages of jumbled, disconnected ideas when you need to focus on a specific theme or plot. Surprisingly, some tutors will go so far as to say that writing ambition can stifle creativity. In *The Writer's Idea Book,* author Jeff Heffron says: *"It's good for any serious writer to understand the marketplace, but writing for the marketplace is a bad idea. If you don't feel passionately about a subject, you won't write well about it."*

I strongly disagree. Most writers attending writers' weekends, conferences and workshops *do* want to produce marketable material and rarely fall into the 'writing for fun' bracket. In my experience, they come to learn how to give themselves the edge over the rest of the freelance fraternity. That isn't to say that they don't enjoy their writing, or refuse to join in the exercises – but it is their very own creativity that makes it fun not the taking part in writing activities.

On the other hand, exercises that are too narrow can also be self-defeating. Creative writing tutorials often set a selection of subjects for students to write about but those setting the course get to choose the subjects. As a result, by the sheer reason of the exercises being designed to stimulate a general cross-section of humanity, the subject matter itself may be restricting, or self-defeating as far as the imaginative/creative process is concerned.

Even if you have no interest in writing for the MB&S market, there could be lots of ideas to be found here to add a new dimension to your characters. Some writers used the characteristics defined by star signs, and most of us know people who read their horoscope every day in the newspaper, whilst strongly maintaining that they don't believe in such rubbish. How many of us were brought up with family customs such as touching wood, throwing salt over the left shoulder, or not crossing knives if we didn't want ill-luck to follow. Superstition still plays a large but sometimes unconscious part in our daily lives, and nearly everyone had a Granny who read the cards or tea leaves: that's why I always include *The Penguin Guide to the Superstitions of Britain & Ireland* by Steve Roud on the writer's reference shelf.

⇨ **What are your family superstitions? Can you use them in your writing?**

Handy Hint:
Don't be tempted to spend money in expensive shops when experimenting with different relaxation techniques. Major supermarkets stock a wide selection of home fragrances, and charity shops will provide a wide range of mood-music. And if they don't work, you can donate them back to the charity shop to benefit someone else. Do try creating your atmosphere with the aid of exercises, fragrance, candles and/or mood music.

- Sit in a comfortable chair with your Ideas Book and a pen close to hand and let your mind run over some of the ideas you've been playing around with for your next piece of writing.

- Single out one of them and visualise the scenario if this were part of real life ... what would happen ... what could happen? Jot down immediately your thoughts and impressions for later analysis.

Try This Exercise:
Take a favourite family superstition and create the opening paragraph to an article, short story or poem around it: even the most ordinary of people refuse to walk under a ladder. Customs and superstitions often vary between the English, Irish, Scots

and Welsh – with even regional differences or rarities to add to the confusion. For example:

- In *my* family, a bird flying into the house means news or a visitor arriving from afar; my friend's mother from Yorkshire believes it to be a death omen! Lots of scope for misunderstandings … and humour.

Chapter Nine

Writer's Itch

"Are we never to have palaces, never to have refined tastes, complex pleasures, never to let the imagination fulfil itself?" **John Fowles, *The Magus***

Secret Step Seven reveals the importance of using our imagination when exploring other artistic mediums such as painting, sculpture, music, etc., because creativity is a state of mind, and the secret is allowing those other influences to stimulate our own creative impulses. Museums, art galleries, historic buildings, stately homes and gardens all provide exceptional stimulation for the writer's 'inner eye'. It may be the ambiance of the place that produces a sense of relaxation, or a getting-away-from-it-all feeling for a few hours, that frees up the brain for creative thinking. Or some fleeting idea that grows into something else.

We can utilise the imagery of a particular exhibit or feature without focussing on the actual story behind the item itself. For example, a previous winner of the Lichfield Prize, Brenda Langmead, based her contemporary family story, *After Lucy,* on the aftermath of a cot death tragedy that had been inspired by the white marble sculpture inside Lichfield Cathedral known as 'the Sleeping Children'. And I've often had an inspired moment during classical music concerts at St David's Hall, Cardiff. It doesn't mean that my mind was wandering away from the music; rather it was in a more receptive state, a heightened level of consciousness *because of* the music.

And interest begets interest. The popularity of the televised Edwardian period drama, *Downton Abbey,* filmed at Highclere

Castle in Berkshire has also apparently benefited other stately homes, the Duke of Devonshire was reported as saying in *The Daily Telegraph*. As a result, and because the 'upstairs, downstairs' nature of country houses has an ongoing appeal, the new visitor programme at Chatsworth now includes a guide posing as a lady's maid, unpacking her mistress's clothes for a glittering Edwardian house party. If we want to write about life in the grand houses, books such as *Below Stairs in the Great Country Houses* by Adeline Hartcup (Sidgwick & Jackson) provide a tantalising glimpse 'below stairs' for the historical novelist.

We may not be able, or want to adapt our ideas on such a great scale, but there may be scope here for some other development. For example, there are about 400 location scouts in the UK, who are looking for potential properties for filming, documentaries, photo- and fashion-shoots, etc. Are there any local stories here that could interest a wide variety of publications? As we've seen from the numerous television programmes on the subject, many of the smaller country houses also have a story to tell – with many diversifying into hospitality and entertainment enterprises to keep the lead on the roof. Investigate the local country houses in your area, especially if still family-owned and there may be an inspirational piece to interest the *BBC Good Homes Magazine, Country Homes & Interiors, Homes & Antiques, House Beautiful,* etc

We may have our own favourite places to go when we make a special trip into town, or take ourselves on a prolonged walk through a park. There may be special exhibits or statuary that we like to visit when we're in the area, almost as though it would be a breach of etiquette not to spend a few moments there. For example, I can never call in at the British Museum bookshop in London without dashing up to the Egyptian Galleries to visit 'Ginger', a pre-dynastic basket burial, even if only for a few seconds. Dion Fortune used the British Museum for the opening chapter of her novel *The Winged Bull*, and even though the internal layout has changed considerably since the book was first published in 1935, the images can still evoke the fog swirling round the columns of the portico and the stillness of the long galleries. John Fowles uses a similar sequence set in the Victoria and Albert Museum in his novel, *The Magus*, when an important point needed to be illustrated in the narrative.

And sometimes, when we've been working too hard, we find our writing isn't flowing as well as it might. So let's give ourselves a break and inject a little bit of 'displacement activity' into our routine. Displacement activity encompasses those things we find to do in order to put off a more important chore, but this time we can do it with a clear conscience. The following is a list of things to take time out to do:

- Visit your local museum or art gallery, and reflect on items of immediate interest in the collection, such as a new exhibit. Is there something here that could be of interest to a regional magazine or newspaper? Can it provide a backdrop for a short story or poem?

- Read at least one book on a subject you've not been interested in before. Is there some snippet that could be incorporated into your 'work in progress' to add another dimension to your writing?

- Visit at least one local historical site (the older the better) and look at it with the 'inner eye'. What is there here that you can use to broaden the interest in your scene setting?

- Visit at least one local beauty spot, or a formal garden, for the purpose of meditation and reflection. Use the opportunity for people-watching, and for material you can include in your writing.

- Treat yourself to a traditional 'afternoon tea' in a local teashop. No reason other than to enjoy a moment of good, old-fashioned luxury and make the day special!

Now back to work ... This kind of picture-play can tell us more about places and the characters who inhabit them than pages of description or dialogue, simply because they can be used as key devices when introducing the good, old-fashioned 'red herring' – or play an integral part in the story, especially if readers are familiar with the scene. One character may, for example, use the subject of a painting as an analogy for the message he is trying to put across to his companion. Watch people moving among the exhibits. Some stand well back with a rapt expression on their faces, while others are drawn to touch the surface of a statue gently with the tips of their fingers, in almost a caress. What is it that at that particular moment, has communicated something inexplicable to these casual visitors?

But this stimulus doesn't necessarily have to spring from anything artistic or cultural, and scene setting doesn't have to be confined to museums and art galleries. Think of the wonderful backdrop of Stourhead Park with its grottos and classical temples; the tropical house at Kew Gardens; or the changing seasons at Wisley. Or more further afield, the natural landscape of the Grand Canyon and Death Valley; a sunset on the Nile and the formidable slopes of K2 in the Himalaya.

Creativity cannot take place in a vacuum and although we can invent a whole community, we need to firmly anchor the action in the reader's mind with the occasional use of real places and/or locations, if only to recall the colour of the beech trees in autumn, or sunlight playing on water. That is why I chose rural Northamptonshire for the setting of my first novel *Whittlewood*; the village was completely fictitious but Whittlewood was the ancient name for the vast royal hunting forest that had once occupied some 32 square miles of the County from medieval times. Although only remnants of the old forest still survive along the old Roman Watling Street (A5), it was where I grew up, and was therefore an area that still retained some of its old magic.

➪ **Creativity is inspired by the right surroundings**

Beautiful Things

When we create fictional people or places for our stories, there is a temptation to cast them all in the 'beautiful' mould. As writers, however, we understand that although there are many things in Life that strike us as beautiful, beauty is most definitely in the eye of the beholder. So what does the dictionary have to say about 'beauty'? According to one of my editions: *That quality or assemblage of qualities which gives the eye or the other senses intense pleasure; or that characteristic in a material object or an abstraction which gratifies the intellect or the moral feeling; a beautiful feature or characteristic; embellishment, grace, charm; a particular aspect that gives satisfaction or (ironically) the reverse.*

From this we can see that beauty does not necessarily have to conform to obvious classical art-forms. Beauty can be in anything and everything: animate and inanimate. It can reduce us to tears; render us speechless, or bring a lump to the throat. No one thing can have a monopoly on beauty and if I were to list those things that I personally find beautiful, the list would be endless. I would have to include favourite poems, pieces of music, certain personal possessions, family heirlooms, my greyhounds ... and that's even before I move into the wider world.

The key-word 'beauty' is a good place to start for a mind-mapping exercise and to see how far we can go with it. Once we've included the obvious personal choices, then moved on to Nature, we find ourselves going beyond the predictable and into the realms of the right-brain. How often have you declared something to be beautiful, only to be met with looks of outright incredulity on the faces of friends or family? This is because we view things with an 'inner-eye' – and the inner-eye is more discerning. The more we use right-brain impulses to stimulate our creative writing, the easier we find it to move away from the 'obvious' and explore the obscure, the outré, and the oblique.

⇨ **Learn to develop the inner-eye to register things that others don't notice, because that's what gives an added dimension to our writing.**

Closer to Home

We don't, however, have to go out into the wider world to find things to write about, and which we find beautiful. Reading through back issues of *The New Writer* and *Quartos* magazines, I came across an article that began: *"I came to freelance writing by way of our house; in fact by way of its collapsing roof. The roof was medieval, listed and covered in hand-cut forest marble stone tiles ... and to replace these, even with grants, was going to cost the earth..."* Hilary Townsend kept the *Quartos* readership enthralled with her horror stories of visiting local authority architects and planning officials. The thrill of the discovery that the property was medieval with Templar connections, and had a Tudor parlour, was quickly dissipated by the restrictions (and cost) placed on the renovations.

As entertaining as it was to read about the old house, the purpose behind the series of articles was to illustrate just how many different types of magazine were interested in the subject, which widened as the work progressed. Not only were there historical magazines, there were also the home and lifestyle publications, not to mention the hundreds of building-trade related outlets. The author dined out on her house for years in terms of hundreds of different articles for a wide variety of magazines and trade newspapers.

Few of us are fortunate enough to live in such a wonderful old property but every period house has a story to tell ... and there are numerous magazines that are willing to print it. Readers (and television viewers) are extremely voyeuristic when it comes to other folks' homes, so there is a very large marketplace for anything unusual or interesting, while several popular television property series highlighted the public's taste for the redecorating follies of the more *avant garde*. But it's not necessary to be outrageous.

- Have you, for instance, spent months trawling round reclamation yards looking for replacement Victorian or Edwardian fixtures and fittings for a house that had them all ripped out when the property was 'modernised' in the 1970s?

- Did you, like Hilary Townsend, come up against the often weird and wonderful planning regulations that demanded that the oak for the replacement medieval staircase had to be imported from the USA! This angle subsequently led to articles for the Woodland Trust and various timber-trade journals.

- Or have you tips and advice for DIY decorators on how to beat the current credit squeeze?

Glossy magazines like *Homes & Gardens* and *House Beautiful* would require good quality photos to accompany your proposal, but the popular women's magazines could possibly be interested in the more domestic hints and tips. Like our medieval homeowner, you could find outlets in the building trade and architectural journals if the problems were of an unusual nature. Don't be afraid to look at the Property pages in the weekend newspaper supplements, since most of these use articles on home improvements, renovation and building problems.

➪ **There's also an occasional opportunity for humour when writing about builders**

Man's Best Friend, and other animals

We all think our own pets are beautiful but if you have an unusual variety of pets, or specialist knowledge about certain kinds of animal, then there are dozens of market outlets for articles on pet keeping, animal husbandry and humour. Sit down for an hour or two in the public library with *Willings Press Guide* and you can provide yourself with enough potential markets to keep you going for a year! Of course there are specialist publications especially for dog, cat and horse owners, but don't overlook the weekly and monthly national magazines that could be interested in material with a slant on animals.

A piece on a PAT dog, for example, would appeal to a wide range of editors from the women's mags to the professional journals. It's just a matter of slanting the article to suit the readership. For example the women's magazine editor would probably look favourably on the owner's story - the care professional would be more interested in the therapeutic benefits. You don't have to be the owner of a PAT dog to write the piece - just know someone who is and be able to produce a good interview.

Be warned, however, very few editors will accept the mawkish sentimentality often accompanying animal features. Include humour, by all means, since animals are one of the best sources of laughter around. Look at the books by Simon Whaley: *One Hundred Muddy Paws For Thought* and *One Hundred Ways For A Dog To Train Its Human* - and the children's book: *Puppytalk: 50 Ways To Make Friends With Your Puppy.* The original idea came from a 150-word filler, followed by a 800-word article. It took Simon several years to find the right format for the first book but his research paid off as the book spent four weeks in the Top Ten Non-Fiction Paperback bestseller list. Six months later, he was advised that the Italian Rights had been sold ... followed by the

Portuguese ... and American Rights. Nearly a year after the launch of the first book, the publisher's children's department asked him to produce a book aimed at 7 to 11 year olds about how to look after a puppy.

As Simon wrote in an article titled 'Animal Magic' for *The New Writer*, *"Animal behaviour is frequently used as a fillers and letters in magazines today, and this was where my first observations were published ... animal behaviour observation is there for any writer to draw on."* Remember that editors always need good, informative and authoritative material by competent writers on animal keeping, whether about six hens in a run at the bottom of the garden, or keeping quail for the gourmet egg market.

⇨ **Animals cover a broad spectrum of the market place and the opportunities are boundless.**

Warning:

(1) In this area of writing the writer will run the risk of editorial prejudice in surprising areas. For example, some equine magazines will not include pieces on hunting or horse racing; while most dog magazines will not feature racing greyhounds - only retired ones. Check previous issues!

(2) Avoid 'talking animals' in your work. With the exception of Suzette A Hill's '*Bones*' series, I can't think of another instance where it's worked in adult fiction, and certainly never in competition. The book review in the *Guardian* (of all places) said of *Bones*: *"Quite why this series should be charming, astringent and witty, instead of emetically twee, I am not sure, but it is entirely delightful."* If you're tempted to give your animals a voice, study this series carefully before starting!

Handy Hint:
Make sure that you always have a current copy of 'What's On' for the area where you live. These publications usually include opening times for gardens and historic houses, theatre promotions, amateur dramatics, concerts and other items of local interest. Lots of potential for articles and interviews for specialist magazines here.

Try This Exercise:
Think of a favourite 'thing' associated with a particular location and produce a piece of writing that refers to it – just a few, short lines. If possible, obtain a photograph, magazine pictures, or re-visit the location and try to look at your 'thing' with new eyes.

- Can you see or feel something different about it that you've never noticed before?

- Can you think of anything you are writing that could take place at this location, or feature the 'thing' you have in mind?

Chapter Ten

Dramatis Personae

> *"When the characters are really alive before their author, the latter does nothing but follow them in their action, in their words, in the situations which they suggest to him."* **Luigi Pirandello**

Hands up everyone who can remember being chastised as a child for having an over active imagination? How many of us will admit to adult day-dreaming that can still create mountains and fabulous animals out of cloud formations, or discover castles and a whole new world in the glowing embers of a fire? Few will probably admit to the latter. I suspect, however, an even greater number will have had those creative impulses 'knocked' out of them by unsympathetic teachers and family members because we were supposed to shape up into prospective 'grown-ups', able to cope with life, not day-dreams.

Unfortunately, those who are sadly lacking in the creativity department see over-active imaginations as a handicap. So, if creativity hadn't been completely dispersed by the time we left school and coped with career and family commitments, then it was kept hidden away as if it were something to be embarrassed about. And yet that childhood penchant for day-dreaming enabled us to create other worlds in which we played the starring role of a hero (or heroine) of the Wild West, Camelot or Battlestar Galactica. As grown-ups, we can now go to **Secret Step Eight** and give our imagination free rein; open up our unconscious minds to the creative possibilities around us and if necessary do the opposite of what is considered the norm ... because the secret is still having the strength to day-dream.

The dictionary defines creativity as: *To cause to exist; to produce, give new form, character or qualities; form anew; to bring into existence; to be the occasion of; to originate; to invest with a new character, office, or dignity. Having the power to create.* It should not, however, be measured by an individual's ability to produce fabulous works of art: a person who organises 'living history' classes in schools is just as creative and innovative as a literary novelist.

By becoming more openly creative, we improve the quality of our writing, and there are almost as many kinds of writing as there are creative people, since it can be expressed in many different ways. Nearly everyone, at some stage of their life, dreams of being an artist, a dancer, a playwright or a writer - and it takes strength to turn the day-dream into a reality. We're never too old to learn how to paint, to dance, or to write - and to break out of the mould we were channelled into. No one says we have to stay there. That we can't break out. Through school-days, career-days and family-days we march to someone else's tune, even though deep down inside we may march to a very different drum. Now it's time to let self-expression and creativity run wild and free ... and create the characters we dreamed of being.

As writers we must develop the knack of creating the right person for the job. All writing, whether fiction or non-fiction is dependant on the people involved – the human interest – those who move the story along; even all-action, plot-driven thrillers require a strong cast if the job is to be completed satisfactory. A great deal of non-fiction writing (especially interviews) involves a human-interest angle, but if we fail to create a sympathetic character within the telling, then the editor/reader will lose interest and move on. It's *people and their well-told stories* that make the writer's world go round, but we still have to work on making those people come alive on the printed page, whether its fiction or true-life drama. Readers usually enjoy a particular piece of writing because they empathise with the character; they see the character in their mind's eye and have little difficulty in stepping into the world the writer has created for them. And it doesn't matter how good your backdrop is if your characters don't pass muster.

So how can we create these believable people?

As writers we must also learn how to coax our readers to step into that dream by encouraging them through the magic of the written word, to suspend disbelief for a little while - just like *Alice Through the Looking Glass.* The same devices must still be used in non-fiction, so that instead of just a dry thesis on fly-fishing, the reader steps into the waders of the *Country Illustrated* narrator with all the attendant sights and sensations of the river. Biography might be based on fact but it would be pretty dull if the reader couldn't step into the glittering world of the celebrity, or back in time to observe life as courtier at the court of Catherine the Great. And for all the popularity of the television soaps, it's easier to get someone to imagine themselves to be a key-player in a 'larger than life' drama than it is to see themselves as the landlady of the Queen Vic! That is why our ideas need an element of escapism, or a sense of the ridiculous: and the ability to work with an outrageous or impractical scenario for our characters that can suspend the disbelief of the reader to such a degree that they don't see the join.

⇨ **Day-dreaming is part of the writer's mental tool box.**

Characterisation

Another word that needs to be included in the writer's vocabulary is 'empathy'. According to the dictionary, being empathic means: *Having affinity with; or sympathy for; like-mindedness; community of interests; fellow feeling. Empathy gives us the ability to understand how other people react, think and feel in a given situation and relate to it in a personal way*. This also gives us the creative insight to be able to 'flesh out' characters and enable us to turn them into three-dimensional personalities, not cardboard cut-outs. This in turn enables the reader to develop an empathy with them.

There's an old 'truth' in creative writing that if we do not care about our characters, then why should we expect our readers to care what happens to them. Good characterisation is the core of all good, readable material - even non-fiction, since especially here, the narrator (i.e. the ghost writer) needs to exploit his or her empathy with the readership of the magazine or newspaper to gain sympathy for the person whom we are writing about.

This is why it is so important to introduce flaws into characters, since we cannot successfully portray characters that are all good, or all bad; complexity in characters should never be under-valued, even in poetry or short story writing. Human nature being what it is, everyone is blessed with both negative and positive traits to their personality. If our villain is an out and out bad 'un, all we are doing is justifying his or her comeuppance in our *own eyes*, not the reader's.

All of us have flaws or faults in our make-up and these should be honestly reflected in the characters we create. People in real life are not drawn in black and white – and neither should fictitious ones. Bishops may harbour murderous thoughts about the Dean; a serial killer may draw the line at destroying a work of fine art. A well-known film producer once told a scriptwriter that he could destroy his visual concept of a vicious hit-man just by having him stoop to stroke a cat on his way to carry out a murder, and without a word being spoken. And even Hitler loved his dog, Blondie. So, let's look at a couple of other contradictions.

From *Wuthering Heights*, Heathcliffe has been the heart-throb of generations of females and yet who, in their right mind, would put up with this kind of psychotic behaviour for one moment. Without putting a finer point on it, Heathcliffe is a monster but his passion raises him above a mere figure of romance. He is like a spectacular comet, which we may admire from a distance, but would decline the opportunity to follow in its fiery wake.

Conversely, Edward Fox in the title role in *Day of the Jackal* is the epitome of the quintessential English gentleman and not a character that one would normally have associated with an international assassin, unlike Jean Reno in *Leon*. Yet the Fox portrayal meant that he'd taken the role right away from the archetypal image we have of such characters, and made the story even more credible because it was so far removed from what we would expect.

Appearances can be deceptive but in fiction it is essential that they *are* credible. In other words, we need to know why a particular character acts in a certain way that appears to be going against the grain of his/her personality. By using the mapping technique to create family connections, we can also come up with an unexpected answer to some of these problems.

Creating a whole cast of characters for our early writing usually presents little difficulty. As we've seen, it is generally acknowledged that most early writing, particularly most first novels, are autobiographical in that main characters reflect the thoughts and reactions of their author. The supporting cast is also readily assembled, drawn from a life-time's garnering of friends, family, colleagues and chance acquaintances. They are all there, filed away in that subconscious zip-file, waiting for us to turn them into fictional (or sometimes non-fictional) players in our drama or romance.

But what of subsequent novels? Or the casting for short stories? How is it possible to create a fresh set of players every time? How often have you suffered disappointment when a favourite author's third or fourth book turns out to be a thinly disguised re-hash of previous characters dished up with a different sauce? Learn from your own criticism of other authors, strip those used and familiar personnel out of your mental files and create a set of new ones.

But where can we find a completely new cast to replace the

ones that took a life-time to assemble? One method is 'casting'. Unless characters appear, unbidden and ready-formed on the page, try to imagine which actors you would select to play the parts if the story were transposed into a film or television script. We usually have a rough idea of what our characters should be like, so we can try to find an actor who has played a similar part, or who would be likely to fit the role we're trying to create. If you feel this idea is far-fetched, admit how many times you've been exasperated by a casting director's decision to cast a particular actor in a part – particularly if it happens to be an adaptation of a favourite novel. All we are doing is reversing the process. It is essential, however, that we develop and extend the personality in our own players, and not rely on merely copying an actor's performance back into the written word.

For example, when author Alan Richardson began writing *The Giftie*, (a novel based on the 17th psychic Robert Kirk), he mentally cast Billy Connelly in the starring role. By the time the novel saw the light of day, his perception of his character had altered and the actor who was now best suited to the part was Johnny Depp. During the years of researching and re-writing, the Connelly image had grown away from the part, while Depp had matured into a fine character actor.

Secondary characters must also be given a life of their own if they are to perform their proper function. The development of their role is just as important as that of the main characters, or they will appear wooden, moving through the plot like puppets. We can't have one dominating set of people with everyone else scooting around on the periphery of the story. As with live theatre, the supporting cast should be there to *enhance* the role of the leading players, not be overshadowed by them. Neither can we give our main characters all the best lines with the rest muddling along as best they can. The arch-master of the supporting role is still Shakespeare, so take a look at how he managed to inject life and dialogue into his sundry players.

➪ **Every character must be there for a purpose and no matter how unimportant their part in the story, there must be a valid reason for them being there - or they should be cut.**

Workshop:
One of my popular workshop exercises requires the collecting of a series of full-page adverts, feature or fashion photos depicting portrait pictures of unknown people from the glossy magazines and weekend colour supplements. Each person taking part in the workshop selects a single picture at random and is then asked to produce the following:

- Two line description of the person in the picture in the role of a hero/heroine.

- Two line description of the same person in the picture in the role of a villain

- Two line job description or occupation of the character

- and lastly, give the face a name suitable to the image

The exercise can produce some hilarious results and the more varied the subjects of the pictures, the more creative the writing. Some fashion-shoot pictures provide period settings, while designer advertising often provides a complete story-line in one single frame. It wouldn't be the first time that a workshop participant had exclaimed: *"That's just the face I want for my novel!"*

Creating a 'Dream World'
In our supportive dream-world we can exploit characterisation to an extreme that would never be possible in life. We can fantasise to our heart's content and choose to surround our

characters with all the things we think would make life more challenging. We can create bizarre situations and exotic locations in our imagination that break away from the stereotypes that frequently occur in popular fiction.

For example, in my current 'work in progress' novel, *House of Strange Gods*, I came up with the idea of using the concept of Frank Lloyd Wright's architectural designs as a model for the house, rather than the usual medieval or Gothic scenario we would normally expect to find in a novel in this genre. Instead of the rambling ancestral pile with its battlements and catacombs, the scene is set in an Art Deco-style building that was created in the 1930s. The strange thing is, that as soon as I started to research Wright's work, I quickly realised that the story just couldn't be set anywhere else. Nevertheless, although it's a story of contrasts, it meant realigning my principal character, because she had to sit comfortably against an Art Deco backdrop.

But to go back to Vivienne Crowley's quote earlier in the chapter: that our dream world has to be so real that the readers want to share it with us. This is why it is so important for our creation to be accessible; it must communicate all the thoughts, words and deeds of the characters, so that our readers *want* to respond to them. Needless to say, it is always necessary to introduce some sort of serpent into this Eden, otherwise the story becomes a cloying world of pink candyfloss and fluffy bedroom slippers.

⇨ **So how do we stimulate this desire to respond? …**

Observation and participation

Imagine a child standing on the edge of a ball game. He or she is an observer simply because, being a new kid in school, s/he hasn't been included. Then someone throws them the ball and suddenly they find themselves participating in the game with all the zest and enthusiasm they can muster. As the child responds, we as writers must learn to throw our readers the ball so that they can join in and be swept away with the narrative.

To participate, they don't necessarily have to be included in the action. A spectator at a ruby match can still participate by actively encouraging his team from the stands; he still shares the exhilaration and frustration of the players on the field even though he isn't included in the action. The letters sent from readers who'd enjoyed *Whittlewood,* all said the same thing: that once started they couldn't put the book down. Because it was a modern Gothic horror story none of them would have wanted to participate in the action, but they were perfectly happy to cheer the main characters on from the sidelines. An observer is merely one who is there for one reason or another, but who is not completely involved. They may wish to join in, but no one ever throws them the ball. As the man said, however, you can't please all of the people all of the time.

As editor of *The New Writer,* I am also fully aware that a proportion of the readership is likely to dislike some of the poems or short stories we publish in the magazine, but that they are still more than likely to submit their own material for consideration. There are others who will never feel like picking up the ball (i.e. submitting material) and eventually they will drift away, and take out a subscription to other magazines with which they may feel they have a greater empathy, or because the 'rules of the game' are perceived as being different.

Question: How do we encourage readers to participate?
Answer: By identifying and empathising with the readership at whom our writing is aimed ***before*** we sit down to create the words.

Taking risks

How often have you had a brilliant idea, only to discard it because it feels unworkable, or worse still, unbelievable? Believe me, this type of idea is worth pursuing – even if you only make a rough outline in your Ideas Book. A germ like this took over six years to grow into *House of Strange Gods*, when suddenly a series of unrelated 'real life' happenings turn fiction into fact, and back into fiction.

Noël Coward knew all about taking risks – but he also knew the value of giving an idea time to breathe. In *Past Conditional* he wrote: *"I knew from experience that once I could snatch out of the air the right ideas for a play, the actual writing of it would not take long. Once the basic theme of a play has been worked out in my mind, I have always written quickly."* It's getting the basic idea that takes the time.

In *Future Indefinite* he elaborated on the subject but added that a serious writer must know when to rein-in the pace of his writing, should it get the bit too firmly between its teeth. *"I am also aware though, from past experience that when the right note is struck and the structure of a play is carefully built in advance, it is both wise and profitable to start at the beginning and write through to the end in as short a time as possible. On the occasions when I have followed this procedure, notably* Private Lives *(four days) and* Present Laughter *(six days), the results have, I believe, justified the method.* Blithe Spirit *was exceptional because its conception was followed immediately by the actual writing of it.* Private Lives *lived in my mind several months before it emerged.* Present Laughter *waited about, half formulated, for nearly three years before I finally wrote it."*

This means having the audacity to give reality a flick of the wrist and send the idea spinning into creative overdrive while keeping it on a lunge-rein. The fully-formed, innovative idea may not materialise immediately but it is important to keep it in some form of perspective, because experimental or audacious writing still needs editor or reader-appeal. The dictionary definition of audacity is: *Bold, daring, courage, gallantry, hardihood, effrontery.* In other words, when you come up with an original idea, push it to its outer limits and explore all it possibilities –

even reverse it, if necessary.

Take a calculated risk with your work now and again, and it might just pay out – particularly when entering material for competitions. In the majority of cases, magazine editors are bound by house-style in what they can accept for publication. Occasionally, they will take the odd gamble with their readers' sensibilities but rarely will it be a departure from their normal publishing policy. Competition readers and judges on the other hand, love to see something new to break the tedium of the hundreds of short stories or poems that regurgitate the same tired treatments. Don't be afraid of taking risks. After all, if your work isn't selling then it may be that a change of direction is needed if you want to realise your ambition to become a serious writer. If you are unsure about a new style or approach, submit the material under a pseudonym and no one will know it's you.

Commenting on the subject of innovation and imagination in *From An Editor's Desk,* poet and then poetry editor of *The New Writer,* Abi Hughes-Edwards said: *"It is possible to treat an common theme in an original manner; a sunset for example, a subject portrayed by many. One can always write about it from different aspects: BE the sunset, what it touches, how it influences, its absence – your loss, etc. Or try writing in a different form, a ballad or sonnet perhaps. Whatever you do, don't write a list of colours. Dulux do that already. The same may be applied to another poets' favourite – the seasons. Why should something as potentially wonderful as the seasons be reduced to a list of climatic conditions? The Met. Office does that: a poet should do more."*

So ... hands up everyone who *still* has an over-active imagination that can create those mountains and fabulous animals out of cloud formations, and discover castles and whole new worlds in the glowing embers of a fire.

⇨ **Now go out and create those characters and worlds that readers will want to visit.**

Handy Hint:
In fiction writing the names of people and places are extremely important, since they convey a lot of unwritten detail about the setting and social standing of the characters. A great source book for this information is *The Oxford Names Companion*, which is a guide to surnames, first names and place names of the British Isles, and should be on every writers' reference shelf.

Try This Exercise:
Baudelaire wrote that *"one must be willing to dream and one must know how."* Write down a 'dream' you'd like to achieve as a writer but be realistic ... there's no point in having a dream about writing a best-selling novel if you've never written a word of fiction before.

- Using the mapping technique and starting with your 'dream' as the key-word, make a list of all the things you think you'll need to do before you can begin to follow your literary dream.

Chapter Eleven

Cruise to Nowhere

"The whole subject of the uncanny is certainly fascinating. And uncommonly good material for imaginative writing. When you come to think of it, all the world's great stories have an element of mystery. Its abandonment means the sacrifice of a great many good story-telling effects." **Suzanne Ruthven, *From An Editor's Desk***

Whatever we write, from romantic novels to popular non-fiction, we still need an element of surprise, if not mystery, to retain the reader's attention. Just as the novelist needs to make sure that the action and characterisation is maintained throughout the story, so too, must the non-fiction writer pay attention to the drama of knowing the exact moment to introduce the 'surprise', and when to reveal the newly researched material. If it has been introduced too early, the reader closes the book with a sense of disappointment and frustration; they learn all there is to know without the need to read through to the finish.

In fact, good non-fiction writing requires all the skills of a novelist in order to maintain the momentum for a full-length book. It doesn't matter whether it's self-help, astronomy or zoology, the narrative needs to be both entertaining and absorbing from beginning to end, with plenty of new information – otherwise, why should anyone bother to buy it? Reveal the full reason for writing it (i.e new information) within the first two chapters and we might just as well prepare a magazine feature, and not bother to create a further 45,000+ words on the subject!

In other words, both the novelist and non-fiction author must know the value of suspense and that, by a general rule of thumb, non-fiction also requires a smooth narrative that flows from the beginning, through the middle, to the end – but with a few surprises along the way.

Phase One:
The beginning introduces the topic under discussion; makes reference to previously published material on the subject including both supporting and opposing viewpoints; but only *partially* reveals the reason behind the writing of a new book. **Mystery.**

Phase Two:
Introduces the new, in-depth research/discovery and brings in generous snippets from previously unquoted sources. But don't be tempted to use all your surprises just yet. **Suspense.**

Phase Three:
Draw together all the loose strands and arguments, saving one or two surprises until the very end. Like the novel, non-fiction should still finish with a bang, not a whimper! **Revelation.**

We also need to look upon non-fiction as a different form of storytelling, and employ the old writers' adage of 'showing not telling' when we wish to reveal another important piece of information. We can overload the text with pages of dreary facts and figures, but it won't enhance our reputation as a writer if the reader develops a glassy stare after the first couple of chapters. And if we're not informing the reader about anything new or surprising – why are we writing a book on the subject?

Neither does modern fiction writing need those long descriptive passages that give everything, except the main character's blood group – because they don't cater for today's reader's love of mystery and action, tempered with brevity. Physical description should only be used to imply personality and/or character, and add a little depth to the storytelling. Today's publisher is more interested in what goes on in a character's head, rather than being told how beautiful the heroine is – so cut the 'shimmering, long blonde hair and sapphire blue eyes' routine and concentrate on injecting a few surprises instead. Rest assured that (regretfully) both Balzac and Dickens would be given short shrift by any editor in today's publishing climate.

Contemporary characters still need an element of mystery, even to the point of being unpredictable, or even volatile. If the editor or publisher's reader knows too much about a character from the start they can become bored and lose interest in the typescript, because where the writing offers no surprises, the whole story will lack a sense of drama. Make sure that the main characters exhibit some form of idiosyncrasy that deliberately or unconsciously arouses suspicion or drama – even if this turns out to be a red herring.

And mystery doesn't necessarily mean anything supernatural or criminal, it can be distinctly domestic in origin. For example: when I was very small I emptied my mother's jewellery box and festooned one of the rose bushes in the garden with the contents. My misdemeanour was quickly discovered but in a very short space of time, the whole lot went missing. A stranger couldn't have taken it because our anti-social dog was on guard in the garden, so it must have been someone she knew. The culprit still remains a mystery to this day.

Mystery can also follow **Secret Step Nine**, by connecting to our unconscious mind and exploring the wealth of universal memories of myth, fantasy and symbolism. Here we shouldn't be embarrassed by our ability to travel to the 'hidden' world, because the secret is being able to channel our favourite childhood images …

The power of mythos

As children we willingly allow ourselves to enter the world of myth and legend; we immerse ourselves so far into these fantasy worlds that we have the ability to become the characters we're reading about. Even as we move through adulthood, some of us often remain locked-in to this world of mystery - as the success of Tolkein's film version of *The Lord of the Rings* has revealed. But what advantage does it give us as writers if we have retained a wide knowledge of the myths and legends of different cultures?

When in doubt, I always refer to the *Encyclopaedia Britannica* because the information is based on scholarly research and not on any airy-fairy theories. So it may surprise us to learn that myth, folklore and legend are now recognised 'as a vital part of the development of the human race', rather than a confused jumble of ancient cultural children's stories. It is also accepts that the roots of mythology and legend have 'a kind of thinking that is not random and which has its own peculiar logic'.

This is not, however, the rational logic that sits comfortably within the remit of modern society. It works through that irritating right-brain maze of analogies, allegories, symbols — all of which means making connections between things that outwardly and rationally are not connected at all. Tales that might, at first glance, seem just childish fancy are far from being merely fanciful and are the means by which the ancient people 'expressed their fundamental notions of life and nature'.

So, when we talk about the 'mythology of Greece' for example, we are referring to the whole host of Greek divine and heroic legends, and to the various attempts that have been made to explain these ancient narratives in modern terms. In reality, the function of these myths was to strengthen tradition and endow it with a greater value and prestige by tracing it back to a higher, better, more 'supernatural' reality of ancient events. It was a technique worked to perfection by John Fowles in his novel, *The Magus*. This also shows that what men have thought, all over the world and all through history, about the supernatural is important, not only for what it may tell us about the mysteries of life and death as the ancients viewed it, but for what it can tell us about human beings today in terms of inter-action, drama and reaction.

From the writer's point of view, we need to put ourselves into the sandals of those ancients who suddenly awoke to the reality that their mysteries were very much in need of explanation. And with good reason. *Britannica* goes on to explain that the myths of the Aryans of India, the Celts, the Egyptians and the Greeks, all contain two elements: the rational and, what to modern minds seems, the irrational. *'The rational myths are those that represent the gods as beautiful and wise; but the real difficulties presented by mythology spring from those irrational elements, which to modern minds appears unnatural, senseless or downright repellent'*. But from all this mystery, myth, murder, mutilation and mayhem springs epic romance and tragedy. Because myth touches the deepest desires of everyone — fears, hopes, dreams, passions, and sentiments. *'Good triumphant over evil validates the social order, justifies the existing social scheme of things and ranges from expressions of sheer artistry to legalism, with its strict adherence to laws and formulae.'* Evil triumphant, on the other hand, merely means that good lives to fight another day.

As *Britannica* points out (and as the writer will quickly realise), behind all this mythical thinking lies artistic or poetic thinking. In this light, it is not surprising that myth and legend have been largely the creation of poets and artists, and that the importance of myths and legends for us is their constant mysterious poetic or romantic appeal. The great classic myths remain 'true' stories; not because we think they really happened but because they contain certain 'universal truths' about humanity and life – and remain an important ingredient in the writer's repertoire of allegory and analogy that can be used to embellish our writing.

⇨ **A modest reference collection of myths and legends from various cultures will certainly enhance the**

flavour of any writer's narrative and the reference shelf should certainly include *Brewer's Dictionary of Phrase & Fable* and *The Oxford Companion to Classical Literature.*

Go with the flow

Going with the flow encourages us to view these creative, subconscious urges as a running river. We allow the current to carry us down stream and along the way we may find ourselves encountering still backwaters, wide flowing basins, white water rapids, and even the Styx or Lethe, to continue the mythical references. This mysterious river, however, isn't all smooth sailing but it travels within the confines of its banks even when running at flood tide; should it break out from those naturally confining barriers, it becomes unmanageable and dangerous.

Admittedly, if we allow the current to carry us along, we may discover other mysterious places we didn't know existed, or look at the view from a different perspective, but if we have no control over our craft, we can be swept out to sea. Very often we begin a piece of writing telling one story and end up with something completely different if we allow the under-current to bubble up from our subconscious mind – that unpredictable and mysterious right-brain again! The more we allow this process to inspire our writing, the more adept we become of knowing when to throw out the anchor; in the meantime let the inspiration of the moment carry you where it wants to go.

Experienced writers also know that writing, particularly fiction and poetry, seems to develop a life of its own and no matter how carefully we plot, the finished piece may bear no resemblance to our original ideas. It is difficult to keep the original idea firmly in our conscious mind while our subconscious mind is going with the flow, but as long as we keep the banks in sight, we can always steer ourselves back to shore – **and know what to edit!**

"Needs to try harder."

Those of us who were chided for having an over-active imagination also probably had this little notation on the term report. As far as the writer is concerned, however, if we try too hard, our imagination refuses to come up with the goods because mental pressure is a kiss of death to creativity. Even experienced non-fiction writers will find that on occasions, the pressure to produce an article takes on an exaggerated degree of importance and, what 24-hours earlier would have been a painless exercise, now becomes an insurmountable problem. The harder we try, the less likely we are to get the thing written to our complete satisfaction before it needs to go in the post.

As we have (hopefully) come to realise, non-fiction writing *is* only a slightly different formula to fiction, simply because the confines of the box are usually much tighter and less flexible. I once had a request for a feature covering the varied approaches between the different pagan religions for a magazine. In order to give each a fair amount of coverage and restrict the piece to 2,000 words was no-go, until I hit on the idea of writing about the different approaches to contemporary pagan death/burial. The finished article was accepted by the original MB&S magazine and later by the *Funeral Directors' Journal*: as a result the funeral industry is now talking to pagan organisations about the difficulties and misunderstandings that have often occurred between them in the past. *Death & the Pagan* was later developed into a full-length book, written under a pseudonym, but it took all the skill of the novelist to make such a serious subject readable.

True creativity is taking pleasure in the act of creating rather than sitting back and admiring the finished product – journeying hopefully rather than the actual arrival. While we are journeying, we are aware of the changes and fresh perspectives that float past and seizing the opportunity to incorporate them into our writing. We don't necessarily need to keep on track, because a detour often means we find ourselves taking a scenic route that hadn't occurred to us before. A large number of authors will admit that they lose interest in a piece of writing once they've finished it; publication is more often than not, an anti-climax.

Writers often find that when working on something that really interests us (such as a favourite hobby or interest, or the action part of a novel), we don't have to think too hard about it. On the other hand, if we become bogged down in an uninteresting bit, the piece refuses to move and it becomes difficult to focus our creative energy to kick-start the process and regain the momentum. This is what happens when people refer to 'writer's block'. What we need to do is some mental re-focusing and find an alternative viewpoint that powers up our creativity again.

⇨ **Get the characters doing something unexpected, or reverse the perspective of the article, or poem – inject an element of mystery or surprise.**

Don't throw it away ... yet!

Having worked your way through this book, you may find yourself thinking that it might be a good idea to junk all your 'work in progress' – and start again from a new perspective. Although it is unwise to become cluttered up with out-dated books and cuttings, half-finished typescripts, article or short story ideas, rough drafts of poems, etc., do think carefully before disposing of any material.

It is rare indeed that a piece of writing can't be re-jigged to turn it into a saleable product. *Signposts for Country Living* was one of those typescripts that had been languishing almost-finished on the hard-drive for several years, and was on the verge of being consigned to the recycle bin. Then, as I've said before, a friend spotted a new publisher and the rest is history; the point being that this particular publisher didn't even exist when I began writing the book.

Another title now under contract was a first draft of a reference book that I'd been compiling for years for my own personal use. It was something else I'd re-read when having a good clear out of the hard drive and around the same time, come across a similar title recently published. Mine – although only a first draft – had twice as many entries. And where as the newly published book was a rehash of information that was so readily available that it hardly needed a dictionary to find it, mine had the weird, the wonderful and the obscure – which is why I'd started keeping records in the first place. The one thing that publishers like is to be able to say is that their book is bigger than your book, so I dusted it off, added an introduction and submitted it as a formal proposal. The result was acceptance with the request to *double* the number of entries, and add 26 mini-features to the finished typescript!

In fact, of the eight new books now under contract, only one was a brand new typescript; another was an out of print book that has been completely repackaged – the others had all been lounging around for years and doing nothing to earn their keep. We all have finished and half-finished typescripts idling away in the computer, and there are probably a variety of reasons why these have never been completed.

- It may be that the content lacks the mystery/surprise necessary to give the narrative an added sparkle; or it's lacking in imagination. We may realise something is wrong, but cannot identify the problem; or know what to do to put it right.

- Or the 'plotting' just runs out of steam … and your how-to becomes a how not to. If characterisation or case histories lack-luster, and are short on human interest/surprises, then the whole thing will come to a grinding halt.

- Perhaps the difficulty was finding a suitable publisher, because sometimes a book is ahead of its time and some won't take the risk. There are now lots of new independent publishers springing up, and a much broader market for the unusual if we do our homework thoroughly.

- Other books may have been in print but had a short shelf-life due to poor sales – but this may not be because there was anything wrong with the book itself. The original publisher may not have marketed it properly, or it may have been a new departure in subject matter that didn't work for them. Have another look at your out-of-print book and see whether it can be repackaged, and resold.

And by re-packaged I mean *completely rewritten* with a bright, new approach including fresh material, language, quotes and anecdotes brought up to date, with different headings and titling. Style and layout constantly change and it is no longer fashionable to have pages and pages of text – today's books have plenty of sub-headings and bullet-points, shaded boxes and listings, etc. So have a rummage through your hard drive and back-up files, and if there's anything that can be repackaged, get it out in the form of a proposal. It really does pay to periodically go back over old and half-finished ideas, simply because publishing is not static and editors move around. You might find one of those old ideas has a sudden burst of life and enthusiasm if a new (and suitable) outlet is discovered. Never throw anything away until you are 100% sure that there is no life left in it, and there is nothing that can be recycled! After all, editors change ... and so does our own writing.

Don't be too eager to discard reference books and clippings either, especially if your subject is historical or political. In recent years we have seen how smear campaigns and media-mongering have altered the face of current affairs. What appears to be up-to-date news today, may be tomorrow's smoke-screen, and adding back-dated controversial comparisons to your topical non-fiction may make all the difference to a commissioning editor.

Likewise, history books that have been proven to be sheer bunkum still have their uses. Because very often those sources were used as school textbooks and reflected the perspectives of the time. For example, using material from *The War Illustrated* (a weekly wartime newspaper) for the background for my novel, *The Wild Horseman*, provided the information that was *circulating during the actual time-sequence of the narrative.* This was later proved to have been air-brushed for the benefit of readers' morale but it was what my characters would have been reading in June 1940.

Conflicting (scholarly) opinions are also a must if you want to add spice to your article in the form of mystery and conspiracy, so even if you think that Richard III really was responsible for the murders in the Tower, most editors would now expect you to mention both sides of the argument. You will need reference books/clippings supporting those opposing opinions if you want to demonstrate how fully you have researched your piece.

A demonstration of history coming full circle is shown by the writings of archaeologist, Dr Margaret Murray. During the 1920s and 30s she published two books on witchcraft, which caused a sensation amongst academics and historians, and for the next 40 years the *Encyclopaedia Britannica* included her entry as proven fact. A third book, published in 1933, however, reversed the scholarly acclaim and her theories were subsequently dismissed as the senile wanderings of a 90-year old crank. Some 80 years later, we are told that Murray's books weren't so far off beam as her critics had imagined.

⇨ **If your writing interests are history and/or politics, be sure that what you are about to throw away really has no life left in it – or you may regret it.**

Handy Hint:
One hint when striving for economy of language, is studying the technique of using names to convey a description of a person, place or thing, whereby the 'name' conveys to the reader much more than a single word. For example, a *Daily Telegraph* journalist described the circumstances surrounding Sam Whaley-Cohen's winning of the 2011 Cheltenham Gold Cup when the amateur jockey beat his professional rivals in racing's most prestigious 'jump' race, as 'epitomising the Corinthian spirit'. Or we might use the term 'Arthurian' to refer to something romantic, mysterious, chivalrous and legendary. A good source is *Name Dropping* by Philip Gooden and published by A&C Black, although there is no reason why we can't coin our own descriptive 'names'.

Try This Exercise:
Think about how your own personal creativity and perspectives have developed since you began rummaging around in the right-brain and giving it free rein. Think about various writing projects that you've abandoned in the past because you didn't get the rush of creativity you needed to complete – or even start – them. How many times have you given up the idea of writing a novel or play, taking up poetry, or writing non-fiction because the creative spark wasn't there? Are you now looking at things from a different perspective?

- List the writing projects you'd like to see through to completion and make a concerted effort to begin.

- Is there anything there that would benefit from an injection of mystery, suspense or surprise?

Chapter Twelve

Have Them Rolling In The Aisles

> *"History has seen more than its fair share of optimists and idealists, but fortunately their baleful influence has been consistently undermined by the remorseless hard work of the cynics. These champions of hard-headed common sense have toiled ceaselessly against anything that smacks of principle, tact, good taste or moral uplift ..."* **DICTIONARY OF CYNICAL QUOTATIONS, Jonathon Green**

It's always been recognised that laughter is the best medicine, and it's probably a rare day indeed if we go through it without something raising a smile. We may be fed up to the back teeth with family squabbles, money worries or ill health but the antics of a squirrel in the park breaks through the gloom. We may be reading a serious book on the train but suddenly the author's turn of phrase makes us laugh out loud and startle fellow travellers. Humour doesn't have to be contrived, stand-up comedy, to make people laugh ... but it does need to create mind-pictures in the imagination of the recipient.

Some years ago, ignotus press received a typescript that had bags of potential. The whole thing was hilarious but unfortunately, the authors had intended it as a serious diatribe on contemporary paganism. They weren't too keen on the idea of the book being turned into humour, but since no other publisher had made an offer on it, they allowed it to go to a ghost-writer ... and the *Coarse Witchcraft* series was born. Esoteric author, Alan Richardson said of the first book: *"It made me laugh out loud in more than a few place. In fact, I think it is the first book of its kind: although it pokes fun at modern excesses and can laugh at itself, it still manages to teach the real stuff at a very high level."*

Craft Working and *Carry On Crafting* were best-sellers for the publisher and although the reviews all echoed Alan Richardson's sentiments, the original authors were still unhappy. Subsequently, copyright for the series passed back to the publisher and the third and last book, *Cold Comfort Coven*, will hopefully see the light of day in the not too distant future. Which goes to show that humour can be found in the most po-faced of situations, and does not necessarily comprise any serious points the author is trying to make.

Lynne Hackles used a similar formula in *Writing From Life: How to turn your personal experience into profitable prose*, by adopting as her motto 'never the let the truth get in the way of entertainment'. In compiling a practical how-to book for writers, she nevertheless shamelessly exploits friends and family to provide original examples of how she turned them into hundreds of saleable stories. Possibly Lynne's secret step is the ability and willingness to laugh at herself, and get the reader laughing while they learn. And her article: 'Warning to all writers – writer's bum', speaks volumes!

When looking for submissions for *The New Writer's* 'Writer's Rant', I'm on the look out for a rant that makes the reader identify with the subject and raises a chuckle. Just like the letter I had from a friend that chronicled her fight with the telephone company and its India-based call centre.

"I've been trying to sort this out since last August, and in that time must have spoken to more Indians than John Wayne! After hanging on for an hour in an attempt to hear a human voice, I've gone through the numbers-game:

Press 1: If you have a morning to waste and you want to feel crap for the rest of the day:

Press 2: If you've lost the will to live

Press 3: If you've died while waiting

Press 4: To be cut off – and now you have four more choices

If you get a ringing tone it's interrupted every 30 seconds telling you that you are in a queue. Hang on for another 45 minutes and then get cut off and have to go back to Press 1 ..."

We've all been there and had our blood pressure raised as a result, but if we're going to convert the experience into a saleable piece of writing it must contain an element of tongue in cheek, rather than 500 words of polemic bombast. Similarly, our Irish telephone system requires you to say 'Help' to pass onto another level, and I've had a neighbour galloping into the house in answer to my call, when roaring 'Help' for the umpteenth time at the automatic answering service. And because we've all experienced similar frustrations, the images or mind-pictures become extremely visual indeed.

And here we come to the last of our secret steps - **Secret Step Ten** – that reminds us of those images or symbols, which open doors to the collective unconscious. When we encounter them during our daily lives, we need to try working with these mind pictures to stimulate our creativity no matter how ridiculous or outrageous at the beginning. It doesn't matter whether you're a poet, short story writer, novelist or journalist, the main ingredient for the majority of our ideas is: people – or more specifically, human-interest.

⇨ **A serious writer is an avid people-watcher – as we've said before, he or she is also an eavesdropper and a snoop – and the secret is focussing the mind on those things that will encourage creative energy. And hopefully make our readers smile.**

Subliminal messaging

The long-arm of co-incidence can often provide material that lends itself to a quirky or humorous approach. Even in the normal course of events, weird co-incidences are always cropping up to give the feeling that there is some outside agency at work over which we have no control. We are aware of the small, insistent voice attempting to make itself heard, but we're not sure of how to receive the messages (or images) it's trying to send. How do we interpret them? Or recognise them?

Firstly, if you subscribe to the theory (as I do) that there is no such thing as co-incidence then it means that those messages *are* trying to tell us something. Tony Crisp, writing in *Coincidences* says: "*When something as strange as a striking co-incidence happens to you, it confronts you with the inexplicable. There is usually no visible links between the event and your environment. A powerful coincidence often gives you no rational clues either, unless perhaps you look beyond logical thought.*" Crisp rightly believes that we should not consign the experience to the past and move on, because the absence of any rational explanation, or easy interpretation, discourages us from further investigation.

From the writer's point of view, a coincidence is something that we feel within us, which then links to an outward event, or vice-versa – and can also be an extremely useful storytelling device for the novelist. We might feel the vague stirrings of an idea but it's so fleeting that we can't pin it down long enough to jot down notes in our Ideas Book. Then pertinent images, pictures or articles appear in magazines or newspapers; a programme unexpectedly comes on television; the idea starts to wriggle around like a ferret in a sack. All these synchronistic happenings suddenly gel together and there's enough to work into a manageable collection of notes and the project is under way.

Even if we've gotten used to logging-in to the right-brain at will, we will still find that impressions come through to us from subliminal levels in other forms, too. In future, it may pay to take a little more notice of them and understanding what those messages may mean. These examples are viewed from less serious analogies:

The Chaos Theory

You know that one already: the idea that a butterfly flapping its wings in an Amazon rainforest can cause a *tsunami*, or tidal wave, on the other side of the world. Mari Messer in *Pencil Dancing* described chaos as 'the space between you and the creative process'. Regardless of our individual beliefs, the majority of people accept the basic concept of the world forming out of the black, watery void that existed before Creation. This void is chaos – and it is out of this 'blackness' the writer begins to see the glimmering of an idea like moonlight shining on dark water. The light is visible but it is too dim, as yet, to see anything by.

When we sit staring at a blank screen waiting to begin a new project and the ideas won't come through, we can think of ourselves as part of this emerging from chaos. The basic life-form of an idea is there but maybe it needs a little longer before we attempt to work on it. Utilise some of the displacement activities described earlier and give the idea a chance to work its way through from your subconscious, away from the physical presence of the computer. Ideas in their embryonic stages are shy, ethereal things and can quickly slip away if startled before they've had time to metamorphose into something more tangible.

If we can recognise when we're at the Chaos Theory stage, we can stop ourselves from panicking that we've lost the knack and merely allowing things to happen naturally. Jot any random thoughts down in your Ideas Book so you don't loose them but be content to sit back and do nothing for a while. Or do something else. When you're least thinking about it, the idea will materialise and you'll be on your way … and it's a much more creative train of thought than merely thinking in terms of the wretched 'writer's block'

Sargasso Sea

This is a tract of the North Atlantic that is covered with floating seaweed; the winds and ocean currents influence its extent and density. Columbus who, on his initial voyage to the 'new India', was becalmed amongst the weed for several days, and the first to report this naturally occuring phenomenon. This area is also known as the horse-latitudes, a region of unpredictable calms on the northern edge of the trade-winds, where it was often necessary for the old navigators to throw overboard the horses they were carrying to America and the West Indies, in order to conserve water.

This state of 'becalmed' is what writers also come up against when they refer to writer's block. They stop halfway through a project and can't seem to get re-started, or can't find the impetus to carry the project forward. Again, if we can recognise the fact that we're in the Sargasso Sea and that sooner or later, the winds will fill our sails and allow us to complete the voyage.

At this stage, however, it might be necessary for you to jettison some of your cargo, even if it means cutting a favourite character or two out of the plot. Try to visualise the part of the narrative where we've become tangled up in the seaweed and try mentally removing a character, or rewind the scene. Can you come at it from a different viewpoint? Or have someone do something unexpected? Think about it on the right-brain level and you'll soon see where it isn't working.

The Enemy at the Gate

In the good old days, when cities were under siege, every bit of man- (and woman) power was needed to repel the invaders. The populace had to leave their trades and professions to man the walls in order to protect hearth and home. When the siege was over and the necessary peace treaties signed, the enemy withdrew and the populace returned to their trades and professions.

The enemy, in this case, can be family, friends and the school holidays. When we're dying to push on with a project it can feel like we're under siege if we are constantly being bombarded by demands from the family. The ideas are coming thick and fast but domestic pressures prevent us from turning on the computer. Time becomes a luxury and we wonder if we'll ever be able to pick up the threads of our *magnum opus*, never mind get it finished.

From the writer's point of view, the 'enemy' will decamp soon enough but in the meantime, keep recording those notes in your Ideas Book. Try to take half an hour for relaxation, even if it's only a soak in the bath, but keep the Ideas Book to hand. When the coast is clear, you can pick up the threads again, but it is important to listen to the subliminal messaging of the sub-conscious mind when it's telling you to back off for a while.

"The Name's Bond, ..."

A writer's name is important. It reflects our personality or our *alter idem*, our other self. This other self (or selves) remains hidden for most of the time, only surfacing when we sit down to write, and for many this is a name by which they have chosen to be acknowledged as a creative writer. The dictionary definition of a pseudonym is: *A fictitious name, especially a nom de guerre. A false or assumed name. A name adopted by a person in some enterprise or action. Nom de plume, pseudonym of a writer.*

There's a rather pertinent story about a now famous actress who, in her early days was unable to get the big break. A friend suggested she changed her name and after a considerable amount of deliberation, settled on one that conveyed the exact opposite of her usual pretty, soubrette image. Apparently, from the moment she 'christened herself anew, a slumbering strength and power seemed to wake in her ... She seemed to be imbued with magnetism and filled with a set purpose'.

A change of name is not going to bring about over-night success but it might add a new dimension to your work or outlook. Fellow writers who work under different names admit that both their personality and style do change when they assume their 'other self'. Writers work under an assumed name for all sorts of reasons but it is worth experimenting with because as another writer admitted: *"My other self is much more adventurous and outrageous than I could ever be. I could never say and do the things my other self does – and without batting an eyelid."*

Warning: Do be careful in your selection of *nom de plume.* Make sure it's one that sits easy on your shoulders and won't be a source of embarrassment in the future, especially if you've changed your name by Deed Poll. Philadelphius Tiggywinkle might initially be amusing for anonymous snippets in a country magazine, but you will look extremely silly appearing as a guest on *The One Show*!

Humour, as we realise, is a *very* personal thing ... some of us are amused by political satire; others adore slapstick. It can range from gentle 'mickey-taking' or manifest as vicious lampoonery but however it is presented, some will laugh and some will find it offensive or silly. Try to think of five writers that have the ability make *you* laugh – even if you're fed up to the back teeth with life, the universe and everything. Off the top of my head, I'd have to go for the following:

Noel Coward's use of language in all his writing may, on the surface, have the brittle delivery of a 1930s dilettante but the brilliance of his sharp retorts and descriptions (especially of people) is as fresh and up-to-date in the 21st century, as he demonstrated in his only novel, *Pomp and Circumstance.*

Billy Connelly's scripts have always maintained a schoolboy way of viewing serious subjects, and can deliver the most shocking diatribe, swiftly softened by his characteristic, nervous chuckle. Even his televised travelogues retain much of that talented delivery that can swing rapidly between the ridiculous and the sentimental without giving offence to either party.

Dad's Army (written by Jimmy Perry and David Croft) is the perennial farce that encompasses every element of British humour, against a serious backdrop of war-torn Europe; it ran for 80 episodes between 1968 and 1977. The Home Guard consisted of local volunteers otherwise ineligible for military service, usually owing to age, and as such the series starred several veterans of British film, television and stage, which gave the whole its faultless performances. In 2004, *Dad's Army* was voted into fourth place in a BBC poll to find Britain's Best Sitcom; in a list of the 100 Greatest British Television Programmes drawn up by the British Film Institute in 2000 and voted for by industry professionals, it was placed thirteenth.

Blackadder (first series – written by Rowan Atkinson and Richard Curtis). Although each series was set in a different era, all followed the fortunes (or rather, misfortunes) of Edmund Blackadder (played by Rowan Atkinson), who in each is a member of a family dynasty present at many significant periods and places in British history. The idea for the first series, which placed a comic slant on medieval Britain., was conceived while both writers were working on *Not the Nine O'Clock News*.

Simon Raven's *Alms For Oblivion* has been described as having 'a distinctive tone – confident, worldly-wise, insolently comic … a highly entertaining narrative style … exciting, sleazy, cynical and funny'. And again it is the brilliant use of language that makes the whole ten books in the series a delight to read.

Now my choices probably won't be yours, and your choices won't necessarily be the same as other readers, but if we're going to have a go at writing real comedy/humour, then we need to study the techniques of those writers who continuously make us laugh. At first glance, my five writers have nothing or very little in common – except for a sense of the ridiculous and not allowing the 'sacred cows' of established order to escape ridicule.

➪ **List your five favourite writers of humour: try to find the common denominator between them and have a go at creating something using a similar technique.**

Writing humour isn't about stand-up delivery and sharp one-liners, it's about crafting a series of happenings that instruct or entertain via the clever use of language on any subject or situation. It doesn't matter how funny the original visual idea may have been, without the *right* language to create the images in the mind's eye, the humour will fall flat.

Handy Hint:
Keep a note of original 'one-liners' that you hear (or overhear) that strike you as amusing. They can add a touch of humour to your fictional dialogue, if the characters are becoming a bit intense. Remember that black humour can creep into any situation and often acts as a safety valve to prevent emotional overload. To outsiders, the black humour of the military and emergency services will appear brutal and unfeeling, but it counteracts the horrors encountered in their job on a daily basis. Also described as gallows-humour, a grim or sardonic phrase in a tight situation can add a new facet to a character's personality.

Try This Exercise:
Not all 'things' in life are pleasant but for the writer there's still some mileage to be gained from reflecting on unpleasantness.

Unpleasant things give a sense of drama or throw up obstacles for the main characters to stumble over. Fiction or drama thrives on the unpleasant traits of the characters, while non-fiction should always be honest about the unpleasant nature of the subject, whether animate or inanimate.

- Negativity has its place in plot and character building, so make sure you use your eyes to see the unpleasant side to life. It can be just as inspiring.

- Pick an 'unpleasant' article from your local paper and write the opening lines of a short story or poem based on the idea.

Chapter Thirteen

Mirror of the Mind

"Your original idea will only be the tip of the iceberg. But by the time you've completed the task you set yourself you will undoubtedly have become an expert on the subject, and this could lead to other things." **Lynne Hackles, *WRITING FROM LIFE***

All sorts of different people want to learn how to do different things – getting a divorce, surviving health scares, business or career advice, self-help and improvement, living and working abroad, acquiring social skills, developing a hobby, creative writing ... the list is endless. And if anyone has ever asked for your advice, then you have a skill to write about. How-to writing can run from an article on how-to organise a successful car boot sale to a full-length self-help book on, for example, *Exploring Spirituality*. Or as one Howopia writer commented: *"A lot of us have expertise without realising it. Put a question about something you know well into an on-line search engine and you'll be surprised how many people have asked the same question before. If other people don't know how to do something and you do – then you could write about your expertise."*

My first how-to book, *From The Editor's Desk,* followed the old adage of writing about what you know and I was editing *Quartos* magazine at the time, with one published full-length book to my name. The aim was to produce a practical nuts and bolts guide to starting a writing career, with plenty of additional advice from other tutors, editors, authors and freelance writers. The spin-off was a series of workshops of the same name that proved to be highly popular with writers' groups. The icing on the cake was that as a result of a successful series for The Welsh Academy, I was invited to become a full member of the *Academi* in recognition of my contribution to literature in Wales.

Branching out into the mind, body and spirit market, the next title was the co-authored *Exploring Spirituality,* which catered for the growing interest in alternative religions and the decline in both traditional religious and spiritual values. This had led to an increasing number of people exploring an assortment of Eastern philosophies and mysticism, not to mention the growth in various esoteric and pagan organisations. The book took the stance that swapping religion wasn't always the answer and that people needed to develop a more realistic view of alternative viewpoints. The spin-off was the eventual creation of ignotus press to promote new writers in this genre.

Having discovered the successful formula for writing and presenting how-to books, the next on the list was *The Good Divorce Guide*. This was more difficult because, not having any legal training it needed to reflect the divorce process from a self-help position, and with as many different viewpoints as possible. I also decided to inveigle the support of a male friend who'd always had a lot to say on the subject of divorce in order to give the book a balanced male-female outlook – and give it male-appeal as far as a readership was concerned. In the end we settled for a book that wasn't just about coping with the legal aspects of a divorce; it also needed to be about forward planning and putting lives back together afterwards ... with a certain lighter touch to make it readable.

> As we wrote in the Preface: *When we first began discussing the most common reasons why people get divorced or decide to terminate a long-term relationship, my co-author said: 'There are only four real reasons – money, sex, bad behaviour and those who should never have got married in the first place.'*
>
> *'You realise,' I replied, 'that your comment has effectively scuppered the first four chapters of soul-sister empathising out*

of the book?'

'Good,' he said, 'the last thing men want is a lot of social chit-chat thinly disguised as meaningful dialogue. We want solid, practical advice along the lines of go directly to jail; do not pass go; do not collect £200.'

The Good Divorce Guide is still in print; stills gets me invited to take part in radio programmes on the subject of divorce; and still earns a modest but regular annual sum in Public Lending Rights from library borrowing. On the other hand, it's never been one of my favourite books.

Next came *Creative Pathways: Freeing the Writer's Inner Voice* to support the increased number of writers' workshops I was tutoring. *From the Editor's Desk* was passed its sell-by date and out of print, and another book was required to demonstrate a different approach to tutoring from those early days.

WLTM: The Dating Game grew out of the long conversations with a friend who ran an introduction agency for country people, and who had a wonderful fund of stories – some hilarious, some sad, others encouraging. We decided to avoid the book of funny stories and again went for a practical guide to agency dating for both men and women, coaxing one of her 'gentlemen' to provide the male perspective. By adopting the womag approach to the subject, we had plenty of support from other agencies; it was also aimed at men and women in the 40+ age range, as we felt these were the people who wouldn't be so comfortable with on-line and speed-dating. Despite a double-page feature in *The Times*, this book wasn't a success, and the reason may have been due to the enormous changes that took place within the industry around the time it was published.

Signposts For Country Living is another step-by-step guide to avoiding the pitfalls often experienced by 'in-comers' trying to establish themselves in rural communities ... written from the country person's perspective. Again, by taking a magazine approach of an informal, inclusive style rather than a patronising catalogue of do's and don't's, we also drew on the experiences of a wide variety of other people to provide humour and anecdote. The spin-off has been a series of country-related articles for *The Countryman*.

The current how-to, *Life-Writes*, is my third creative writing book, and has been written to coincide with my acting as commissioning editor for Compass Books, so that as an author there was something new on offer and not stuck in the time-warp of previously published stuff.

As we can see from this small personal selection, how-to books can cover every aspect of life - family, hobbies, career, life-style – and our expertise is drawn from our own experiences. The particular hook (or spin) that we put on the narrative to cater for a specific target market, however, will depend on where we see ourselves fitting into the picture. For example and again using a personal standpoint:

- My three creative writing books have become more ambitious as my own writing career has expanded and developed.

- *Exploring Spirituality* reflected the uncertainty that many people face when confronting their religious faith, and not feeling comfortable with it. It was a subject that cropped up frequently at MB&S workshops.

- *The Good Divorce Guide* couldn't be written from a legal standpoint, so it had to give the message of 'under-standing, coping, communicating and moving on'.

- *WLTM: The Dating Game* was aimed at the middle-age group (men and women) who were hesitant about approaching a dating agency, despite the statistics that one in five adults now use some form of introductory serve to help them find a new partner.

- *Signposts For Country Living* appealed to the publisher because it wasn't written with a rosy hue by townies moving to the country; the authors were country people telling town people how they would be expected to behave this the new environment!

It's not enough to write on a subject with mere enthusiasm because all how-to, self-help and self-improvement topics need to reflect 'life as it is lived' by those who have lived it. My experience as a commissioning editor and contributing editor, plus several other titles in publication give me credibility in the readers' eyes for the three books on creative writing. *Exploring Spirituality* reflects the journey I had made many years before, including the problems and difficulties experienced by the many people I talked to along the way: not to mention the numerous titles published in the MB&S genre. *The Good Divorce Guide* and *Signposts For Country Living* came from experience, and although *WLTM: The Dating Game* was compiled from the experiences of others, the bulk of the material came from a *bona fide* member of the industry, who approved the final draft.

⇨ **All proposals in this genre require impressive curriculum vitae to back up the claims of the author, because readers don't want to be told how to do something by an amateur, or someone lacking the credentials the content suggests – hence the extended Introduction at the start of this book!**

Synopsis and Full Chapter Breakdown

Once we've started to develop the idea for a how-to book, that's when we start to trawl the marketplace for a suitable outlet.

Because how-to publishers usually have their own formula dictating how the text should be presented, and it's not a good idea to present them with the complete typescript, since this may require a complete re-write to comply with their individual house-styles.

This is where we do our homework and investigate every publisher in the genre who is likely to be interested in our subject. This exercise is two-fold because it:

- Identifies the publishers whose listings are compatible with our subject matter and whether there is anything similar already in print.

- Gives an insight into the competition together with the various approaches to the subject already in print.

As we would expect, there were numerous books on divorce but most were written from the legal perspective, so our book covered the shock effects and aftermath of the separation-divorce process. There were several biographical books covering the dating industry, so our book was specifically aimed at the forty-plus age group that made up the bulk of clients in the more traditional agencies. This was due to the fact that middle-aged people are less likely to frequent pubs and clubs, and have little opportunity to meet a prospective partner in their daily routine. There have also been dozens of books about moving to the country but none written by country people for the benefit of 'in-comers'.

This is the information that needs to be included in a synopsis. A publisher needs to immediately see the proposed 'hook' to be able to judge whether the idea appeals, and if the book has a place on their titles list. In other words, show that we've done our homework prior to making contact and prove that we are professionals, not someone working our way through the handbooks.

By now we should have the book mapped out on paper (or computer) so that we have a rough idea of where we are going with it. There should also be a bulging file of cuttings, information sheets and statistics to support our research, and enough time spent on the project for us to be able to prepare a full chapter breakdown. As an example, I have included the chapter breakdown for two of my books:

The Good Divorce Guide

Chapter One:
Knowing the Facts and Exploring Attitudes
Statistics
What the experts say
How did we get to this?
Where did it go wrong?
Being open and honest
Taking the first steps
The warring factions
Considering religious difficulties
When all else fails
Can we take control?

Chapter Two:
Finding a Lawyer
Making decisions
The 'Special Procedure'
When a dispute arises
Mediation and 'fair witness'
Finding the right (wo)man for the job

Signposts For Country Living

Chapter One:
The Country Dream

Getting away from it all
Changing your lifestyle
Working from home
Self-sufficiency
For …
Against …
Village or town?
Or a weekend cottage?

Getting your priorities right
Highways and byways

Chapter Two:
Finding A Home
Deciding on the right area
What kind of accommodation?
Long distance family
How to view
Possible problem areas

Talking it over with a lawyer
How much will it cost?
Being on the receiving end
Changes and quirks in the law
How does it affect you?

Chapter Three:
Legal Mud Wrestling
Keeping control
'When the gloves come off'
Seconds out ... round one
All's fair in divorce and war
Pre-nuptial agreements
Financial settlements
Pensions
Cohabiting
Changes in the law
How does it affect you?

Chapter Four:
Telling the family
Telling the children
Who gets the children?
The absent parent

Telling your parents
A family affair
The friendship factor
On a 'need to know' basis
Spending holidays alone
Asking for help

Child Support Agency

Buying an old house
Sounds and smells
First impressions
Problems waiting to happen
What if …

Chapter Three:
Change of Address
Countdown to completion
Channels of communication
Removal firm or DIY?
The emergency box
Moving in
Covering all eventualities
Stress management
Coping with children
Coping with pets
Your new life

Chapter Four:
Integration or Alienation?
Re-inventing yourself
Fools rush in
It's where you do your shopping that counts
Fund raising
Footpaths and bridle ways
Modernised or brutalised?
The grapevine
'Don't call us …'
A little bit of mystery does no harm
Having a sense of humour helps

Chapter Five:
The Judgment of Solomon
The financial reality
Splitting up the home
Who gets the dog?
Shared business interests
Friends & Enemies
It's different for men
The clock is running
Thirty...
Forty...
Fifty...

Chapter Six:
Dealing with Difficult Partners
Violent partners
So why don't you leave?
Breaking the ties
Protection
Control freaks and drama queens
When it all ends in tears
Men behaving badly

Women behaving badly
Counting the cost
Picking up the pieces

Chapter Seven:
Setting Up A New Home
Buying or renting?
Putting distance between you
The older you get

Chapter Five:
Livestock and Locals
If it's got fur or feathers – it bites
The class(less) system
The village idiot
Making the right approach
Free range animals and children
Acquiring livestock
When to say 'no'
The fox and the hen house
This little piggy went to market
And a pony for the children

Chapter Six:
The Social Scene

The pub
The church
The village hall
The school
The Women's Institute

The County Show
Cheap holidays and Bank Holiday weekends
Go on a treasure hunt
The car boot sales
Farmers' markets

Chapter Seven:
Country Pursuits and Pastimes
Action man
The cricket club
Keeping an eye on the ball

Moving on out, moving on up
Change of address
Financial responsibilities
Furnishing on a tight budget
Managing on a reduced income
Telephone life-line
A matter of willpower

Chapter Eight:
Setting Yourself A Goal

Getting rid of unwanted baggage
Getting on with the job
A change of image
Realising a dream
When in doubt join something
New horizons

Where did it go wrong?
Redefining relationships
Can't help loving that man
There's a whole new world out there

Chapter Nine:
Building The New You

Fuelling the body
How healthy is your diet?

Keeping healthy
Rest and recuperation
Fuelling the mind

Taking time for your life

Huntin', shootin' and fishin'
The village fete
The Game Fair
The answer's a horse
The point to point
Fornication
Politics and the Parish Council

Chapter Eight:
Back to Nature

If it's got fur or feathers – it bites (again)
Being realistic
Don't pick it!
Going green
Growing it yourself
Brer Rabbit and the vegetable patch
The bird table
Rats!
Beautiful but deadly
The Good Samaritan

Chapter Nine:
Long Winter Nights

Absent friends
Log fires and frozen water troughs
'It's haunted you know …'
The 'street light' debate
Space, freedom and independence
When boredom sets in

Rediscovering yourself	Do something you've always wanted to do
Relaxation and quality time	Starting your own business
Self-understanding and self-esteem	Phone the Samaritans!
Downshifting to a richer life	The winter drinks party
Chapter Ten: There is Life After Marriage	**Chapter Ten: Country Reality**
What the experts say	Define your new priorities
Having fun	Reality v. Illusion
From new beginnings	Legislation
WLTM—Would like to meet	Financial considerations
Going on the first date	We couldn't live anywhere else'
New relationships and re-marriage	When age begins to tell
Safeguarding your assets	A richer life
There's no fool like an old fool	When dreams turn to ashes
Redefining you goal	Back to town
Pause for thought	A few final words of caution

Compare the two listings and we can see that the whole content of each book is mapped out from beginning to end. This exercise is dual purpose because not only does it give the writer a clear working plan to follow, it also tells a publisher at a glance, exactly how the completed book will pan out. By preparing a comprehensive breakdown for each book well in advance, we also know exactly what extra material is required, and where it will fit into the text. I've sold all my how-to books on the strength of a good chapter breakdown.

The next step is to study the back-list of all the how-to and self-help publishers who may be interested in our proposal. Try these for starters and obtain writers' submission guidelines for each one:

- How-To Books
- Teach Yourself Books
- John Hunt Publishing
- Aber Books - Studymates

Check out the latest how-to and self-help titles in your local bookstore and library, and see how each one prefers the typescript set out to fit in with their individual house-styles. All of them will require that the author has practical experience in the field in which they write but often this is the first step on the publishing ladder for a large number of new writers.

⇨ **Jot down in your Ideas Book all the things that you could turn into a self-help or how-to book.**

The Spin-Off

Once our how-to book has been published there are various spin-offs that will help us promote sales and earn higher royalties. Magazine and newspaper editors will be more keen to accept article proposals from an author whose book has just been, or is about to be released, because the publisher's acceptance is an endorsement of our writing ability. This can be a feature in the form of an extract from the book, or a shorter article quoting from a single chapter. Needless to say, an editor is hardly likely to make any payment for the piece since it is an extract and not 'previously unpublished'. Nevertheless, it is well worth the lack of fee in order to get our name (and book title) out there amongst the reading public, especially in specialist magazines where there is a higher rate of interest in our subject and people likely to buy the new book.

We can make money, however, if our filler or reader's letter doesn't rely on our book to sell the idea. These small snippets of how-to and self-help advice are popular with editors, and although we won't earn a fortune, 'every little helps' as that supermarket giant frequently tells us. Although some publications pay for fillers and letters, many give prizes that have been donated by advertisers, which can be worth a lot of money. An established writer of my acquaintance submits these for fun and manages to provide all the family birthday and Christmas presents from her 'winnings'. And if you don't want the prize, you can always flog it on e-bay. Trawl the relevant magazines and newspapers for suitable or compatible outlets,

Don't forget the US and UK on-line sites that specialise in how-to material. My bit of fun is Howopia, a new sort of website, that encourages the sharing of information 'for the masses, by the masses'. For example:

How To 'Age' Garden Ornaments

If you want to get rid of that 'straight from the garden centre' look about your pots, tubs, containers and statuary, there is a simple way to age them – naturally!

1 Mix the soot and yoghurt at the rate of one tablespoon of soot to one small pot of yoghurt. This should be sufficient for one good-sized container.

2 Paint the mixture onto the container and leave to dry. If it rains before the mixture is dry, the yoghurt will wash off and the process will need repeating.

3 If the container or statue is made from reconstituted stone and is rough textured, work the bristles of the brush into all the cracks and crevices.

This treatment will darken the 'stone' instantly, as well as encouraging moss and lichen to grow. Using plain yoghurt will not darken the stone, but it will cause it to change colour. The treatment will not work on plastics tubs and containers.

The Howopia goal is to create the largest number of How-To's on the internet – and they pay a share of the advertising revenue generated through the guides we write. The earnings are potentially limitless, and the more pages we write, the more money we can earn. Log on and have a look at how easy it is ...

The Writer on Radio

A word of warning – don't be flattered by sudden requests to go on radio on the strength of your newly found status as a how-to author. It's not that useful ... there I sat, waiting for the phone to ring, so that I could take part in a live radio interview for BBC Newcastle. The programme was scheduled for 11.30 am and had been set up the week before via several emails and telephone calls.

I was due to take part as author of *The Good Divorce Guide* and in trying to get a hook on the type of questions that would arise presented something of a problem because a) the programme makers hadn't even seen a copy of the book and b) it had been written ten years earlier and I'd moved on quite a way since then! The half hour show went off okay but as it was a dual interview with a divorce lawyer plus musical interludes, my input only amounted to about three minutes of air time and featured my personal opinions rather than any real (i.e. useful) reference to the book or its content.

This wasn't the first radio interview I'd been asked to do for this particular book — there had been several others when it first came out. The common denominator was the fact that *not one* of the programmers/presenters had actually seen the book, never mind read any of it.

The most recent request was an interview for a local MB&S radio station that came from my publisher, with a view to marketing my latest title to a like-minded audience. Again there was a flurry of emails and an extended telephone call to try to get an idea of the type of questions they would be likely to ask.

There's a good reason for this ...when you've written a full-length book some 12-18 months previously, it's not always possible to have total recall for every chapter, and a rough idea of the opening questions enables the author to give sensible, confident answers. Again the presenter admitted that she hadn't even seen a copy and hadn't got a clue what it was about! As a result, although the interview was arranged, it never came to pass because the radio station failed to follow-up on the appointed day.

The initial response to a request for a radio interview is one of being flattered but in reality unless the whole programme is devoted to you as a writer, it's unlikely that you'll get any worth-while publicity for your latest publication. And the subsequent reaction to being told that the presenter hasn't even looked at the title, is 'what the hell am I doing this for!'

Handy Hint:
If you think you have the makings of a self-help or how-to book, record your ideas in the form of a 'chapter breakdown' – even if there isn't enough for a full-length book, you'll still have plenty of material for articles, fillers and readers' letters. Remember that each one of your chapter breakdown subjects should be an article in its own right.

Try This Exercise:
Using the how-to example above, go onto the Howopia site at www.howopia.co.uk and see how the published articles have been presented. My articles, as you will see, are taken from my personal interests of creative writing, greyhounds, gardening and self-help. Study the guidelines and write a couple of your own using the accepted format. You can either send these to a magazine (and wait weeks for a response), or register with Howopia, submit your how-to, and get an answer in a couple of days.

- I use this as a system to keep the brain ticking over when I'm working on a full-length book. I look at anything and everything as a potential how-to piece.

Chapter Fourteen

Mother of the Muses: Mnemosyne

"Education, the great mumbo-jumbo and fraud of the age, purports to equip us to live and is prescribed as a universal remedy for everything from juvenile delinquency to premature senility. For the most part it only serves to enlarge stupidity, inflate conceit, enhance credulity and put those subjected to it at the mercy of brain-washers with printing, presses, radio and TV at their disposal." **Malcolm Muggeridge, in the *Observer*, 1966**

Sooner or later, most published writers will try their hand at tutoring. Some are good at it; others dismal failures. Those that are good will have the ability to stimulate enthusiasm and creativity in their students; the 'others' will put the blossoming writer off for life. Some workshops cater for a writer's ego; the best cater for the would-be writer's needs. Sooner or later, the would-be writer decides to invest in a writers' workshop ...

I tutor one-day workshops for my local writers' group, and it's very interesting what they have to say about tutors who've been there before as guest speakers. *"We like you,"* said the organiser, *"because if someone's work is rubbish you tell them so in such a nice away that the writer isn't upset or offended, and the rest of us benefit from the mistakes."* Apparently, one 'guest' had so publicly brutalised one lad's work that he left the group and his mum says he's never written another word. Since he was an absolute beginner – a fact that the 'guest' was made aware of - the group thought this was unnecessarily heavy-handed. Another disappointment was the playwright who spent the entire workshop telling the group how clever and ingenious he was in constructing his plays. The group thought they were going to learn about the craft of playwriting.

These are not uncommon occurrences but it is extremely difficult for the new writer (or even a more experienced one) to gauge whether a particular event is right for them. We can bite the bullet over wasted money if an evening lecture is a disappointment, but if we've shelled out a lot of hard-earned cash for a weekend, or week-long event, then we might be excused for coming away more than a little miffed if the tutoring hasn't come up to expectations. So ... what should we be looking for?

- Don't be tempted by 'big names'. Sometimes the most famous writers don't make the best tutors. Those of an older generation may not even remember what it was like to be a beginner.

- If you are a beginner, make sure that the content of the workshop is geared towards writers who are just starting out. And remember, we all have to start somewhere.

- Listen to the recommendations of those who have attended different events before. Ask what they liked about each workshop, and why.

- If you've got a little bit of experience under your belt, choose a speciality workshop that caters for your particular type of writing. It's no good going to a romantic fiction workshop if your interest is science fiction or westerns.

- Make sure you get the level of tuition that is appropriate for your own level of writing. It's pointless attending a master-class if you've barely managed the first few chapters of a first novel.

- Workshops that request a sample submission in advance of the event will probably offer a harsher degree of criticism, so if you can't stand the heat – stay out of the workshop!

- Be prepared to participate! This doesn't mean you will be expected to perform in front of strangers, but it will mean taking an active part in discussions and exercises in order to bounce ideas off other participants.

I've enjoyed tutoring at various different workshops over the years (including the prestigious Cheltenham Festival – literary not horse racing) but the three that remain firm favourites are the Writer's Holiday at the University of Wales, the Welsh Academy and Horncastle College. The common denominator being chemistry: the right blend of ambiance, enthusiasm and fun.

Top of my list is the Writer's Holiday, a week-long feast of workshops, lectures and entertainment, catering for every level of writing experience – and where the tutors mix freely with the participants out of workshop hours. There are fourteen different courses, which allow you to follow two specialist workshops during the six days, together with a host of lectures taking place during the afternoons and evenings throughout the conference, as well as numerous after-tea sessions, talks and discussion groups on a wide variety of writing-related topics.

The Welsh Academy was a summer-long series of one-day workshops in remote libraries and community centres all over Wales that normally didn't have such opportunities arranged for them. It remains a favourite because, as I've already said, as a result of its success, I was invited to become a full member of the *Academi* and is one of the high-lights of my career. Horncastle College offers workshops on specific subjects – i.e. novel writing, non-fiction or poetry weekends, and I tutored there several times, enjoying the hospitality and relaxed atmosphere of the venue.

⇨ **Ask other writers for their preferences before making your decision.**

What's In It For Me?

I can remember one weekend workshop where we were talking about things that stimulated ideas or interest in us as individuals. It was a good, lively group with plenty of sparking between the participants – except for one chap. He maintained he'd been writing (unpublished) short stories for years but nothing appeared to interest him. He didn't watch people, television, go to museums, the cinema or read newspapers. His imaginative powers were almost non-existent and the group (very generously, I thought) took it upon themselves to help him.

Without being intrusive, they asked questions, made suggestions, took it in turns to include him in their group sessions. They generally went out of their way to find ways of sparking his creative urge, even to the detriment of their own involvement in parts of the workshop. He merely looked bewildered, and hadn't got a clue what we were talking about when he was asked to look at certain pictures and give his own interpretation of the story behind them. I thought it was very sad that he wanted so much to be a writer and yet hadn't got the vital spark necessary for creativity. It reminded me of the old Zen poem:

When one looks at it, one cannot see it;
When one listens for it, one cannot hear it;
However, when one uses it, it is inexhaustible.

Which just about sums up the mystery of creativity. We can't see it or hear it, but once we learn how to plug in to our right-brain, there is an inexhaustible supply of words and pictures just waiting for us to use them.

Another negative occasion was the chap who'd brought along

three novel drafts and expected me to read all of them. Needless to say they were awful and certainly not with any hope of interesting a publisher. Not only was he deaf to any constructive advice, he was extremely disruptive when other people's work was being discussed. There subsequently followed a letter of complaint to the workshop organiser about the harshness of my criticism. It transpired that he had mental health problems and was encouraged to 'write for therapy' but his care worker had failed to communicate this important piece of information and he was treated exactly the same as any other workshop participant – with disastrous results.

It's also been my experience that a lot of would-be writers 'only write for pleasure' whenever their own work is being discussed during workshops. And since I'm not a therapist, I'm not interested in trying to help those who do not want to ultimately aim at being published. If we considered enrolling for a professionally run workshop, then we must be prepared to take the constructive advice and criticism of the tutor, since that's the whole reason for being there.

On the plus side, as writers generally work alone, it makes a refreshing change for one week (or weekend) each year to be in the company of like-minded people, with all our meals provided. Let's face it, we don't often get the opportunity with family and friends to discuss the intricacies of creative writing and a 3-4 day workshop gives us the opportunity to come away with lots of new ideas, as well as tips for improving our existing work.

⇨ **One week at Caerleon and I come back with dozens of fresh ideas, even though I've been tutoring!**

The Sacred Flame of the Muse

If you decided to go to a workshop, do leave 'the Muse' at home. Despite its creative imagery, we need to understand that the 'muse' is not some diaphanous-clad outside agency which hurtles down from Parnassus crying *"It's for yoooou!"* and handing over the idea for next year's Booker Prize.

We also need to accept that 'waiting for the muse to strike' is a universal myth, as literary agent, Mo Sherrard-Smith wrote for *From An Editor's Desk. "Yes, writing may be inspired, but it should be inspired by the author's dedication. That dedication has to come each day when the writing is in progress. How many novels would be written if the Muse had to be summoned and the author had to wait six months because she was on holiday?"*

Each individual's muse is hidden away in the right-brain where the flame of creativity burns bright. Let's go back to the dictionary and find out all about Muses and musing. When we're talking about *the* Muse, we're not talking about any old Muse, we need to get down to specifics and decide exactly which one of the nine daughters of **Mnemosyne**, goddess of literature and the arts, we are calling upon. We have:

Clio, muse of history, the patron for historical writing (both fact and fiction), biographies, memoirs and nostalgia.

Euterpe, muse of lyric poetry, and possibly romance.

Thalia, muse of comedy and idyllic poetry, might help out with humour and playwriting.

Melpomene, muse of tragedy, is the girl to call upon for all types of drama.

Terpsichore, muse of music and dancing, could lend a hand on reviews and interviews in this area of the arts, or a choice of background music for inspiration.

Erato, muse of amatory poetry, inspires erotic writing required for a variety of fiction imprints and magazines.

Calliope, muse of epic poetry, ideal to have on your side if writing a series of books.

Urania, muse of astronomy, can help when it comes to the mind, body and spirit genre.

Polyhymnia, muse of singing and harmony, could stimulate ideas for song lyrics, or for other writing based on song titles.

And according to the dictionary, muse means: *To ponder, to meditate upon; to study or reflect upon in silence; to dream, to engage in reverie; to wonder; abstraction of mind.* It is obvious that there's either the option to sit and wait for the Muse to fit us in to her sacred schedule, or we tune-in to the inner recesses of our own right-brain and go looking for ideas for ourselves!

Handy Hint:
No one is ever too old (or experienced) to learn; and writers are learning all the time. Unfortunately, the local library or Internet doesn't always provide the right sort of material for research purposes and book buying can be expensive. Check out ABE-Books on the Internet at www.ABEBooks.com for second-hand and out of print titles at a fraction of the cost. When starting off on a writing project, I go straight to ABE and can usually find four or five books for about £10 (plus postage) rather than paying full price, and it doesn't break the bank if I junk them at a later date.

Try This Exercise:

Author and creative writing tutor, Sally Spedding uses this technique:

"When beginning a new session with new members I ask them to list six of their greatest fears and six of perceived joys. Next, they are asked to list the six most upsetting/traumatic experiences they have ever had. After this they write six of their happiest experiences. Already we are digging into imagination and experience, so the next step is to ask the participants to write 'what if?' against each of their statements. This flexes the imagination and invariably several interesting plot possibilities emerge, with inherent opportunities for conflict ..." from **WORDSHOPS, Steve Wade**

Chapter Fifteen

Token of Remembrance

Memento Mori: a human skull or any other object serving as a reminder of the inevitability of death. ***NIL DESPERANDUM*****, Eugene Ehrlich**

Where would Agatha Christie novels and the televised *Midsomer Murders* be without an ever-increasing body-count? Bodies from war-zones or natural disasters, murder and mayhem in urban surroundings dominate the lead features on our nightly television news with teenage girls abducted, and madmen going on the rampage with a shotgun. We live in violent times – in reality *and* in entertainment.

As a writer's tool, however, death has produced quite a few monsters of its own. From the gratuitous violence of Micky Spillane's Mike Hammer, who is as psychotic as the villains he eliminates; to the sophisticated executions in the world of James Bond. And probably more poetry has been inspired by death than any other human condition; never mind the best-selling *Angela's Ashes* and *The Oxford Book of Death.*

I can remember my English teacher at junior school having 'quiet a word' with my mother over my choice of poetry. But she only had herself to blame, since we were given a free hand in making our own selection to read to the class. This wasn't learnt parrot-fashion, gabbling and mumbling, and boring the rest of our classmates to tears. This was learning to read aloud, articulating the words and projecting the voice – which is why addressing a lecture theatre full of writers at the Writer's Holiday held no terrors in later life.

The subject of my teacher's concern, however, was a ten-year old's discovery of those arch-priests of the Victorian (albeit American) death cult, Henry Wadsworth Longfellow and Edgar Alan Poe – Bram Stoker came much later. The weekly renderings of *Dirge Over A Nameless Grave, The Beleaguered City* and *Burial of the Minnisink*; or *The Raven, Lenore* and *Annabel Lee* were not deemed suitable class reading.

It was her fault, too, that I was introduced to Shakespearian tragedy early in life. The class was carted off to that wonderful old theatre at Stratford on Avon for a matinee of one of the Bard's comedies but there'd been a change of programme, and we landed up watching *Pericles, Prince of Tyre* instead! I can't profess to have completely understood it at the time, but I've been hooked on Shakespeare's tragedies ever since. The literary horrors of *Titus Andronicus* probably led to a life-long love of the macabre, and eventually writing for the Gothic Society's magazine, *Udolpho* on a regular basis. Or as a friend once observed: " and this from someone who's idea of light entertainment is *The Duchess of Malfi*!"

On a more human level, I've always been a great fan of the broadsheet obituaries, and find a lot of ideas for characters among those illustrious dead. Apart from the rich and famous, the most interesting to read about are those who probably spent most of their lives as ordinary people, but with extraordinary tales to tell. There are war heroes, daredevils, charmers and villains, all of whom have played their part in the history of the 20th century – and a prime example of literary suggestion appeared in the *Daily Telegraph* in April 2011.

"John Hobbs, who has died aged 64, emerged from the demi-mode of postwar west London ..." The obit went on to described him as a 'youth of striking beauty' whose rather chequered career as an antiques dealer cast him in a real-life situation similar to Ian McShane's television role in *Lovejoy*. Like the television hero, he mixed in all sorts of company from housebreakers and pimps to high society, but Hobbs eventually faced professional disgrace

and financial ruin when he was accused of selling fakes. He was also no stranger to literary caricature since Nell Dunne had also used him in her best-selling novel, *Up The Junction* (1963); he was working on his memoirs entitled *Honest John*, when he died.

So how can we use such a character in our story? For example:

- Real people can have walk-on parts in a novel to give it an added dimension, or interest.

- They can play a part in a novel set in the Swinging Sixties – or as a cameo in a contemporary story relating to a suspect piece of antique furniture.

- Create a similar *Lovejoy*-type figure to provide the humour/intrigue.

- Or a revelation in a set of memoirs – Hobbs only discovered 30 years later that he was the father of a grown up son by one of his lady friends.

- The character moves between shady junk shops (Hobbs' father's shop was called Odds & Hobbs), and grand houses in London and abroad.

- Create a character of great charm but with a 'self-destructive personality and a gambler's disregard for the consequences', together with a battle with drink, drugs and depression.

All this information was culled from the obituary, and were we to decide to use a character like this in our writing, then the newspapers of the day can provide even more background material. We are not writing about the person in the biographical sense, we are merely basing a fictional character upon the known background. We can't say with any certainty that John Grant (under the pen-name Jonathan Gash) based his series of *Lovejoy* novels on Hobbs but there is more than an element of suggestion in his fictional character's persona.

Lovejoy was a popular television adaptation about the adventures of a British antiques dealer based in East Anglia, whose scruples were not always the highest. He had a reputation in the trade as a 'divvie', someone with an uncanny talent for recognising treasure, as well as being able to distinguish fakes and forgeries. Add to this charisma and the ability to inspire great loyalty; a talent to mix with the highest and lowest of society; together with the signature black leather coat and we could be forgiven for thinking that John Hobbs *was* the inspiration behind Grant's run-away success.

But a literary death isn't always intellectually appealing. How many generations of children have been emotionally scarred for life by the shooting of Bambi's mother ; or the horrific demise of Ginger in *Black Beauty?* And on the other side of the coin, there are many who share Oscar Wilde's widely repeated criticism of the death of Nell in *The Old Curiousity Shop* that *"One would have to have a heart of stone to read the death of little Nell without dissolving into tears ... of laughter."*

In the midst of Life we are in death ...

When tutoring my novel writing workshops, one piece of advice I give to kick-start a troublesome typsescript is to introduce a body. This doesn't have to be the result of violent crime, it can be natural death due to old age (*Chocolat*), or illness in someone young (*Steel Magnolias*); a tragic accident (*Summer People*), cot death (*East Enders*), or suicide (*Peyton Place*).

In other words, we don't have to be writing a murder mystery or thriller to exploit our readers' reaction to the subject, and an unexpected death in the narrative helps to create a sense of deep emotion and high drama in the gentlest of fiction. It gives a reason for irrational or unacceptable behaviour and misunderstanding; helps create or solve a mystery; or brings out the best/worst in a character. For example:

- When an elderly family member dies a disturbing secret is discovered among their personal papers ... The death might have occurred some time prior to the start of the book; or a funeral used as the excuse to bring all the characters together. There are all sorts of trivial skeletons in closets and bureaux that can rattle a family's equilibrium without being criminal or life-threateningly scandalous. It might even provide a short-cut in the narrative and get the creative ball rolling again.

- The death of a young person, whether family or friend, can be unexpected or as the result of a long illness or suicide ... but it can be a device to bring people together, or drive them apart.

- Accidents can happen to anyone but in order to create a drama and inject emotional reactions into the story, it needs to happen to a prominent character, not someone who's been introduced into the narrative with the sole idea of knocking them off. And it doesn't have to be a dramatic accident to cause family problems. My partner is a work rider within the horse racing industry and has suffered dozens of injuries during his career, but he broke his neck falling down the stairs putting up Christmas decorations! It wasn't fatal ... but it could easily have been ... and the aftermath still caused a lot of family friction.

- Cot death is an emotive subject as the reaction to the *Eastenders* scenario showed when the scriptwriters introduced it into the weekly soap. So many people complained that it resulted in over 8000 viewers taking exception to the way it was handled. Any death – and people's reaction to it – has to be convincing.

- Suicide is another emotive subject but the reasons behind it can add a lot of depth to a story because there will be a long build-up to the actual act. Lots of room for emotional and mental turmoil, but we must avoid a sense of justification, or analysis. People aren't always in a rational state of mind when they take their own lives.

- And let's not forget that for a lot of people, the death of a pet dog is on par with losing a family member, but we have to be careful this doesn't slide into mawkish sentimentality.

Needless to say, it isn't possible to just produce a body in order to kick-start a story. We need to go back and scatter clues and red herrings into the narrative, even if the actual death comes as a shock to the reader. Look at your novel with fresh eyes and see if you can use this device to tighten the emotional screws on your readers.

⇨ **Who can you kill off in order to produce the greatest dramatic impact?**

Death Comes as the End

Or rather the beginning - because in fiction, its purpose is often best served if it occurs *even before the story has started*. No need to get bogged down in the details, these are allowed to surface as the story develops.

The most well-known example is, of course, *Rebecca* by Daphne Du Maurier. The deceased former wife dominating the whole story from beyond the grave; and it was only through the skilful handling of the plot by the author that prevented the rest of the cast from paling into insignificance. Rebecca wasn't a ghost but she continued to 'live' in the minds and memories of all those who had met her, with unfortunate repercussions for the new wife at Manderley. The drama is played out by the characters who are left and who remember her so vividly.

In Agatha Christie's *Five Little Pigs,* it was a murder case that was officially closed with the trial, conviction and sentencing of the victim's widow some sixteen years earlier. Now the grown-up daughter of the pair has come forward with a letter that hints at her mother's innocence, and so the surviving characters are required to go back into the past to relive the crime and its aftermath.

In the highly popular television series, *New Tricks,* the Unsolved Crimes unit are going back through cases up to twenty years old. The team is made up of an ambitious female Superintendent and three former detectives who retired some years previously, which creates the opportunity for some brilliant non-PC moments and prompted the critic from the *Guardian* to write: *"Fresh, original and funny ... for a masterclass in effortless character acting, look no further."*

For the purpose of our exercise, however, we will shy away from the crime/thriller genre and see how we can use the technique in ordinary fiction – both novels and short stories. Most people of a certain age have already experienced the death of someone close, or of someone we used to be close to in the dim and distant past. For example:

- Grandparents
- A classmate while we were at school
- A former school friend
- An old boy/girl friend from our teens
- A former lover
- A flatmate from our twenties
- The person who gave use our first job
- An old business acquaintance

- A sporting team-mate
- A neighbour

Use your imagination to create a scenario whereby something from the past and relating to the deceased, is suddenly catapulted into the here and now. How could the death of someone ten … twenty … thirty years earlier cause problems for us in the present? What can trigger strong memories of the past? Not the spectre of murder but unsettling enough, perhaps, to cause problems, misunderstanding or recriminations.

Death as it is lived …

Death also has a large part to play in non-fiction and if we look at the self-help genre there are numerous titles dealing with bereavement, not to mention the countless articles appearing in magazines that tell us how to cope with the loss of a loved one. *Dogs Today* even has its own pet bereavement counsellor writing a regular column offering advice on how to prepare and come to terms with losing a pet; Laura Lee also wrote the full length *Absent Friends; How to Cope with the Loss of a Treasured Pet.*

Although death stalks us all, the ways of coping with the eventuality vary from person to person. A father will look upon the death of a daughter differently from her mother, and will cope with the tragedy on a different level of emotion. Even siblings may view the death of a parent from differing viewpoints. Our grief can often be gauged by the amount of guilt we feel when someone dies – and guilt can be a very destructive emotion. Was there something we could have done or said to prevent it, or make things easier? Does guilt provide us with a sub-plot for our story?

This is why there is such a wide market place in the women's magazines for articles dealing with the subject. Because if your experience makes someone else say: *that's how I feel,* and identify with your loss, then you've lessened the feeling of isolation.

Editors of magazines and self-help publishers are always looking for well-written human-interest stories, and the approach to coping with death is no exception.

Death & the Pagan on the other hand, was written to offer practical advice not only to pagan families but also for members of the caring professions and the funeral industry. Unless specific instructions are left as to the type of funeral that is required, the arrangements become the responsibility of the executors or family, who will do what *they* feel is right.

It is probably fair to say that the majority of pagans would prefer some form of 'natural burial', and fortunately this is something that is also becoming more and more popular with mainstream belief. Even up to ten years ago, natural burial would still have been considered suspiciously 'alternative' but with the growing awareness of carbon footprints and a spate of celebrity funerals where they had opted for natural burial, the concept is now socially acceptable. As a result and as I explained earlier in the book, *Death & the Pagan* grew out of an article written for a journal of the funeral industry.

But even death has its own gallows humour. We recently had Finn, a greatly loved greyhound put to sleep and when the vet phoned to say that that the ashes were ready for collection she said brightly: "We've got Mr Kelly's ashes here for you."

"I hope not," I replied, "I'd brought in the dog!"

Handy Hint:
Make a point of reading the obituaries in the broadsheets. The majority of the recently deceased aren't celebrities but they have led the most amazing – and often heroic lives. There are so many stories just waiting to be told that involve unknown men and women, but whose remarkable exploits will trigger ideas for fiction and non-fiction. Cut out and keep those that interest you the most.

Try This Exercise:

Create the opening to a piece of writing with death as the main theme. Draw on personal experience, or from something you've read in a newspaper, and write the first two paragraphs of fact or fiction – or opening lines of a poem. Use your imagination to turn reality into a saleable piece of work, because it's quite possible to produce emotive writing without infringing upon anyone's grief or privacy.

Chapter Sixteen

Scraping the Bottom of the Barrel

"Biography, like big-game hunting, is one of the unrecognised form of sport, and it's as unfair as only sport can be." **Philip Guedalla, Supers and Supermen, 1920**

When we run out of our own ideas, we can always turn our attention to the lives of others. And we don't need to be an expert on a chosen subject to produce a saleable interview ... although a little knowledge helps. Saleable interviews, however, aren't necessarily with the rich and famous. Every specialist magazine editor will be interested in sparky interviews with those who participate in that particular subject, career, sport, hobby or profession.

Unless your prospective interviewee is a family member, friend or acquaintance, however, it's advisable to make contact with the targeted editor before approaching anyone with a request for an interview. Most people will ask where and when the finished piece is going to appear, so you'll need an answer ready. Send a proposal to the editor in the same way you would submit any article proposal, with the additional 'carrot' that the interviewee has just completed the New York marathon, won a prestigious award, written a book, etc. Look at the chat-shows on television, nearly every one will feature someone who is about to launch a new series, book, film or show and the lesser celebs are no different when it comes to publicity. We just need to find the right target-market for our piece.

- Having secured your appointment, turn up on time and looking professional.

- Don't waste time with unnecessary chit-chat, you're there to do a job not begin a meaningful relationship.

- The important thing is to have a list of questions ready when you go to the interview, arranged in the order you want to ask them.

- The order in which you want to write them up is irrelevant at this stage, but experienced journalists ask inoffensive questions until the interviewee feels relaxed and safe, and go onto the critical subjects later. One unwelcome question at the beginning may ruin the rest of the interview.

Don't even think about writing up a Q&A interview - it's the mark of an amateur and incredibly boring to read. This format tells the reader nothing about the interviewee, since most of the standard answers can be found in a dozen other similar pieces. The secret of the good interview is to make the subject come alive against a casually mentioned backdrop. I cringed recently on reading that one interviewer had asked George Clooney what his favourite colour was! Gorgeous George probably kept on smiling but we can only image what his private thoughts were ...

For ideal subject matter begin by looking closer to home:

- Local free-papers will give details of people who have recently done something interesting, so be on the look-out for potential interviews you can sell to national or specialist publications.

- Heart-rending local stories might miss the national news but weekly magazines such as *That's Life!* and *Take a Break* are always looking for true life drama.

- Consult the local 'What's On' listings to see if there is a new production, sporting event, or fund raiser that can be reported on for specialist magazines.

- Listen to local radio for interviews that might be worth pursuing.

- Attend local agricultural shows and county fairs, and be on the lookout for material that might suit national farming or country magazines.

For the best examples of how to interview, study the celebrity features in the weekend colour supplements - particularly the *Telegraph*. The more famous your subject, the less you need to spend on personal description because the reader will know what they look like, so concentrate on personal mannerisms, and dress sense, instead. The colour supplement interviews create a whole atmosphere with a few carefully placed thumb-nail sketches of the subject's home, appearance and manner: **read, study and observe**.

Questions relating to well-known facts are permissible but imagine what the champion jockey will think of the journalist who asks: *"In which races have you ridden?"* Try a slightly different approach: *"Which win gave you the most satisfaction?" "Why?"* etc. Ask for their opinions on everything and the stronger their views, the better. Remember that asking 'open questions' that cannot be answered 'yes' or 'no', result in spontaneous answers that make for better material. *"What has been your most nerve-wracking moment?"* invites a better answer than: *"Were you nervous riding in the Grand National?"* This approach is what makes an interview come alive but if you don't understand an answer, it is better to ask immediately for clarification than to 'phone up afterwards.

If you agree (or disagree) with your interviewee's opinion, resist the urge to say so. Your subject may have continued talking and you may lose the original quote you'd been after. *Don't ever mention your own opinion.* If you agree with your interviewee, the interview gets boring; if you disagree, you spoil the atmosphere and, either way, it's wasting precious time. A well-prepared interview of 30 minutes provides ample material for a 1000 word feature, one hour should be the maximum if you have several markets in mind.

Be flexible about the unexpected turns a story may take; some of your questions may turn out to be a dead-end, while your writer's instinct will suggest new angles. Most people are helpful and eager to impress, although some will ask questions to test your knowledge and possibly undermine your self-confidence. Simply ignore them, even if you know the answer, and continue. You are the journalist - you ask, they answer.

- Write the interview up as soon as possible, while you can still read your notes and while your impressions are fresh.

- You will not be able to use all the interesting information you have, at least not in one article. Concentrate on one aspect for each publication.

- It's acceptable to shorten answers, restructure sentences, drop repetitions, correct the grammar and rephrase certain answers so that they read better.

- Don't be tempted to change the tiniest bit of *meaning* - you will be in deep trouble.

- Some interviewees will ask to see the feature before it goes into print. If they insist, offer to read it out to them on the telephone. They can then correct obvious misunderstandings, without a chance to consult anyone.

Of the hundreds of sporting interests, for example, you can guarantee that every one has a magazine to cater for sportsmen and women at all levels of competence from National Hunt racing and snow-boarding to table tennis. Your own blend of journalism and sporting interest will govern the level of the publication for which you can realistically write. Editors are generally looking for experts and active participants, although the enthusiastic amateur might just get the occasional break if you just happen to be in the right place at the right time.

- 'Sports widows' often find themselves in print when coupling their 'how to cope with an absent husband etc' together with appropriate humour. One 'shooting widow' got herself accepted by a predominantly male oriented shooting magazine by providing a few sensible recipes for the 'boot' [For the uninitiated, this is a lunch/picnic served from the car boot.]; sailing/boating publications are always particularly sympathetic to the 'galley slave' on board a Sunseeker.

- Some sports magazines have been known to run the odd short story providing it has the right sporting connection – these are usually short twist in tale or ghost stories. I've even spotted the latter in *Practical Fish Keeping.* Sporting history can also find a niche but do try to link the piece with an anniversary or modern comparison/event for extra editor appeal.

You don't have to be an expert to interview a sporting personality but it helps to have a bit of back-ground knowledge of the sport, otherwise your questions will lack reader appeal. The higher the profile the less likely the fans will want to know his favourite colour (*a la* George Clooney), or what she watches on TV. The writers' handbooks don't list a fraction of the hundreds of sports-mags in the market place, so this is going to be a real research project. Here's where to start:

- Scan through copies of the sporting magazines in your local newsagent.
- Spend the time in the doctor's or dentist's waiting room checking out the sports-mags.
- Ask sporting friends which magazines they read and ask to borrow a few back issues.
- See if there are any spare copies available from your local sports shop.

Sometimes it's necessary to obtain quotes from experienced people to flesh out an article or feature, to give it added depth and editor-appeal. And the way we use quotes can alter the whole focus of the article, because we are using them to endorse or dispute the subject of the piece. Editors of literary magazines are often bombarded with emails requesting us to complete a questionnaire from students studying for a MA in creative writing – no one minds answering questions as one liners but I've received several recently that demand much more! Most editors will dash off a spontaneous reply but it's asking a bit much of anyone to assume they have the time (or the inclination) to answer reams of questions from an unknown emailer. Sports personalities and theatre people will react in the same way, so restrict the answers to one liners unless there is an offer to expand on that.

One the other hand, if you fancy yourself as a sports reporter, offer your services as a village correspondent for local free papers. This might cover football, cricket, hockey, tennis … and if your children attend a school with strong sporting interest, the newspaper might be persuaded to run a regular piece. What about mini-interviews with the local bowls team or the martial arts club? This sort of freelance writing will probably only pay in pence per word but it's a good place to start and gets us used to working to editorial deadlines and going out meeting people.

The Ghostess With the Mostest ...

Although the term 'ghost writer' conjures up thoughts of the supernatural, it's a recognised publishing term that been around for a long time. In general terms, it usually refers to a competent writer, with a proven track-record, who is commissioned to write a book anonymously, so that some 'celebrity' can put out a novel or autobiography, under their own name. More specifically, it can also cover the editing skills that an experienced writer can offer in order to hone and sharpen an existing typescript. Type in 'ghost writer' into your internet search engine and see what comes up.

In the good old days, a publishing house would employ a 'ghost' to refine a promising writer's text. Then, they would think nothing of taking on a 4000-page typescript and pruning it down to a compact 400-page novel. Not to mention the famous Hollywood ghosts, who made countless over-night revisions to film scripts. And a lucrative profession it was, too. In other words, to quote from the *Wikipedia,* a ghostwriter is a professional writer who is paid to write books, articles, stories, or reports, which are officially credited to another person. *"Busy celebrities, executives and political leaders often use ghostwriters to draft or edit autobiographies, magazine articles, or other written material. While some celebrities or well-known figures use ghostwriters very discreetly, without giving them any credit; in many cases ghostwriters are credited as 'contributors', or 'research assistants', or thanked in the preface."*

Ghostwriters are commissioned for a variety of reasons. Publishers may decide that there is a market for a particular autobiography but the celebrity may not have the time, or writing skills, to produce a 300-page book. An experienced ghostwriter will know how to structure and edit the text, so that it is fast moving and holds the readers' attention. They do most of the writing themselves and carry out extensive research using concepts and stories provided by the 'credited author' in their particular field of expertise, in addition to interviewing colleagues, friends, family. They should also be prepared to find interviews, articles, video footage to supplement any material provided by the credited author. It helps, of course, if the ghostwriter has some background knowledge of the author's life or environment, because they can spend anything from several months to a year researching, writing and editing the typescript.

The flat fee for hiring a professional ghostwriter is in the region of £5,000 to £12,000, although the fee for one who has produced best selling books for high-profile celebrities can be considerably more. And in many cases, the ghostwriter may be asked to sign a nondisclosure contract forbidding them from revealing their part in the production of the book. As *Wikipedia* concludes: *"The role of ghost-writers has long been a well-kept secret in the publishing industry; in the 2000s, it is becoming more common for celebrities who have published autobiographies or memoirs to acknowledge the assistance they got from their ghostwriters."*

In the case of the sporting biography, *Champagne & Slippers,* I found myself faced with the prospect of writing the whole book based on information, stories, notes and videos provided by the 'author'. In view of the political climate and the ban on many fieldsports, it was difficult to know what style to adopt - colloquial, humorous, serious, etc. In the end I decided to let the author's voice speak for itself and the tone of the narrative quickly took on the easily recognisable, self-deprecatory style of a man comfortable with laughing at himself. It was heartening to know (once the book came out) that both family and friends felt his 'voice' had not been obliterated in the editing. All I'd done was clean it up!

Before starting on the job, I'd spent a lot of time reading similar autobiographies by other sporting personalities, and was appalled by the triteness of the narrative, which made the 'author' appear more like a half-wit than a sporting hero. A friend in the know told me that a lot of sporting biogs are ghosted by sports-hacks and so the tone isn't very far removed from newspaper reporting, rather than serious journalism. The books sell because they are by (or about) a sporting hero, but often lack the staying power to keep the reader enthralled by the 'story'.

In her latest book, *Ghostwriting – how to write for others*, published by Studymates, Lynne Hackles, says that after much research, poking around, asking many people many questions and generally being a nuisance she is ready to share with all the knowledge she's gleaned, together with her own personal experiences, and those of other ghostwriters. *"I have discovered that there are far more openings for ghostwriters than I first thought. Ghostwriters have been used in the past for writing autobiographies, books and speeches but the market is expanding every day, thanks to the internet, and ghosts are everywhere, busily clicking away at keyboards, writing everything from adverts, poetry, articles, novels, children's books, memoirs and celebrity life stories. Every day new markets for ghostwriting appear on the internet. It's becoming big business and there's no reason why you shouldn't have a piece of it. Any book that you pick up, on any subject, could have been ghost-written."*

Ghostwriters are usually employed by publishers with well-known celebs on their list, whose name alone will sell a book. But not every-one has a riveting story to tell. A couple of years back another friend was commissioned to 'ghost' an unofficial biography of a pop icon. There were lots of videos and press clippings but the 'subject' completely lacked substance. Once the initial scrapbook collection was out of the way, there was nothing to draw on and, because it was an unofficial biog, friends and family of the star were not willing to cooperate. In the finish it turned out to be a glossy picture book because the 'star' was too young to have any real story to tell, and their life was just a series of venues and photo-calls. "Never again," was the verdict on that one, especially when the publisher reneged on the original deal.

Writing someone's else's story is a huge responsibility. I personally wouldn't take a commission if I hadn't got some knowledge of, or an interest in, the subject matter. Having grown up in the country I'd a close up and personal approach to field sports and so was able to understand (and interpret) the jargon for the lay reader. That extra bit of familiarity can be of tremendous help when you're trying to fill up the pages without s-t-r-e-t-c-h-i-n-g the text to fit the target wordage. This meant that the author could sit down and tell his stories, which I could then slot into the text where it would gain the maximum impact often saving some of the best until last. Needless to say, there were a lot of arguments about what should go in and what should be left out. It's not easy for a non-writer to understand why a particular piece can jar on the reader in chapter five, but sit quite happily in chapter eight.

I can honestly say that ghosting that book was the hardest writing challenge I'd ever faced. It called for a different kind of discipline but at the end of the day the glowing reviews in the major sporting magazines said it all. One monthly glossy even published a five-page extract. The book itself sold out in hardback within four months and has now gone into paperback, so the publisher is pleased. All of which looks good on the c.v.

Would *I* do it again? If it was the autobiography of someone who was engaged in an area of activity I knew something about, then the answer is 'yes'. And that, I think is the secret to successful ghosting, like most areas of writing - writing about what you know. The best moment, however, was at the book launch when the credited author introduced me to everyone as: *"This is my ghost writer"*. As it was, the book was nominated for the William Hill Sports Book of the Year in 2006, and who knows, perhaps one day the British Book Awards will come up with a prize for the ghostess with the mostess.

➪ **Make sure you will have enough material to ghost write a full-length book of 45,000 words before accepting the commission.**

... then there's always biography.

Or even faction. From time to time we come across personal stories that hold more than a degree of fascination for us, and this may lead to an inspired piece of writing. Some writers choose to tell the whole life story in the form of a biography; others create a novel based on the factual events of that particular person's life. And, although it is not possible to libel the dead, as writers we do have a moral obligation not to besmirch that name or reputation.

Biographies about non-famous people, however, are notoriously difficult to sell to mainstream publishers, and it is probably a good idea to try and sell the idea before putting in too much work on researching the subject. We have all met people in our lives that make us think: *"What a great story that would make!"* but the publishing industry may not agree despite the fact that our subject might have led a remarkable life. Although people like reading biographies, publishers don't seem to like publishing them ... unless it happens to be about some A-list celeb.

One of the most successful and surprising best-sellers to come under this umbrella was John Berendt's *Midnight in the Garden of Good and Evil*, subsequently made into a film directed by Clint Eastwood. In the first edition, the author included a note to explain that although he'd cast the book in the form of a novel, it was a work of non-fiction: all the characters were real and their stories true. The note appeared at the end of the book, and as a result 'quite a few readers were half-way through – or even finished it – before they realized that what they'd been reading was journalism, not fiction'. So skilful was Berendt's storytelling that in the end, it really didn't matter that the real-life drama of a murder trial was part of a travel book!

If you feel that there *is* enough material available to create a full-length, page-turning life story, write the first three chapters and prepare an in-depth synopsis, stating whether you have access to original sources. Do your homework and ensure that the publisher of your choice has accepted biographies of lesser personages in the past.

⇨ **Use some of the material to create articles that can be aimed at specialist editors, who may be keener to accept life stories in their particular sphere of interest.**

Handy Hint:
If you find something useful in a book, make a note of the page number against the title, otherwise it will mean reading the whole book again to find it. We think we'll remember but we never do. Better still, put a small coloured post-it note in as a book mark so that you can go straight to the page when you need the information. There's nothing more certain to kill creative spontaneity than having to spend hours searching for a single line quotation in a 300-page book.

Try This Exercise:
Conduct an interview with a member of the family or a friend with a view to having it published in your local newspaper or regional magazine. Who do you know that could provide an interesting interview? What about any of the following?

- A successful charity worker
- An unsung hero

- A sporting personality
- A local artist, actor, musician or writer
- A high achiever in business
- A new business venture
- Behind the scenes (theatre, cinema, etc)

You may not get paid for your efforts but it will be your first by-line as an interviewer, and may lead to other things.

Chapter Seventeen

Call Back Yesterday

"I am of a generation that grew up as a teenager in the Fifties, in that repressive, respectable, squeaky-clean, boring ... suburban world. We screamed and screamed, and couldn't get out quick enough." **Dramatist and director, Mike Leigh**

Although at times, Life seems to be permanently set on fast-forward, there is still a lot of opportunity for writing about the slower days of the past. And we only have to look at the number of magazines catering for self-sufficiency and gardening to see that there is still a great demand for the more relaxed lifestyle – and much of it influenced by the past. There's also a renewed interest in country crafts and it's perhaps a bit of an awkward question ... but where does nostalgia begin and memory end?

Short-term Memory

Gone are the days when editors would settle for some mawkishly sentimental piece about days-gone-by; today's nostalgia has become much more practical and informative. There's still plenty of memories and history there, but articles tend to have a much stronger link to the present. For example, rather than recalling how our grandmother made her own butter when we were children – we must now expand the piece to include someone who is doing exactly the same today to cater for a new generation of foodies. In other words, we need to think then and now, rather than writing solely about the past.

By rule of thumb, articles should be about the people and places: places of natural beauty, towns, villages and traditions, any odd customs, legends, folklore, and surviving crafts.

Customs, legends and folklore will have more editor appeal if these can be linked to a modern festival, fair or annual observance. Towns, villages and beauty spots can possibly be linked to something of specific interest for the visitor – a good restaurant or hotel - especially if there is something else of importance going on in the area. Surviving crafts need to feature those working them today, in addition to the historical context.

A handful of magazines immediately spring to mind: *Heritage, Evergreen, This England, Best of British, Beautiful Britain, The Oldie* and *The Countryman* and although each editor welcomes nostalgia pieces, each one has its own distinct approach to the subject. Check out the internet for the individual websites and if it looks like a promising market, acquire several back issues for comparison. Articles tend to range from 500 to 2,000 words, and because they're so popular with writers, you may have to wait up to 12 months before you see the piece in print.

Although the nostalgia magazines *may* appear to be very similar, each one has very specific guidelines:

- *Best of British*, for example, has a wonderfully diverse mix of subjects from the 1940s, 50s and 60s, such as 'your first job, first romance, wartime memories, railways and aviation, TV and radio of years gone by, schooldays, fashions, fêtes, festivals and church hall hops, places to visit and books to read – the list is endless!'

- *The Countryman* is one of the oldest countryside magazines in the world and is read by over 80,000 people throughout Britain and overseas, focusing on the rural issues of today, and tomorrow, as well as including features on the people, places, history and wildlife.

- *This England*, also with a strong overseas readership, is a 'celebration of England and all things English', with regular features including Exploring England's Coastline, A Taste of England, Forget-Me-Nots, Poets' Corner, A Royal History of England, Our English Heroes etc.

- From the same stable comes *Evergreen* a 'miscellany of this and that and things gone by which takes readers on a gentle journey around the highways and byways of Britain'. It explores the countryside, ancient churches and unspoilt villages, quaint customs and curiosities, and shares stories, snippets of poetry and the words of half-remembered songs with readers all over the world. 'There are regular trips down memory lane, with refreshing recollections of Britain in days gone by: fondly remembered summer holidays, visits to the village shop, favourite entertainers, memorable local characters ...'

- *Heritage* magazine describes itself as 'celebrating Britain's rich past and historic present', aiming at the visitor by featuring landscapes of diverse beauty, history and legend' and guides to ancient city streets and county highlights.

- *Beautiful Britain* features landscape, culture, heritage, wildlife, food and travel. Every issue contains 'interesting and thought-provoking writing, in-depth interviews as well as topical and inspiring stories' about the people, landscapes, heritage and events that shape Britain today.

- *The Oldie* is described as a general interest magazine for the older person and 'antidote to youth culture'. Not the usual run of the mill nostalgia but it regularly features, such as an 'I Once Met' column, where readers write about their encounters with the famous or infamous; 'Still With Us', which catches up with people you might have thought

> were dead, and the 'World's Worst Dumps' slot, where readers reveal their most horrific travel tales.'

Each magazine has its own website where you can see what's been included in the back issues. Many of these magazines also have a world-wide distribution so there's plenty of opportunity for overseas visitors and ex-pats to share their (or their grand/parents') memories of old Blighty, providing they fit within the current guidelines. Try to collect a sample copy of each magazine and compare the differences and similarities before sending off any proposals.

Nostalgia is generally thought of as memories that other people can share; excursions into the past that strike a cord with those of our generation, which can raise a smile or cause a tear. But an editor still needs something 'extra' to help them choose my piece over yours. For example: recollections of summer boy scout camps aren't an unusual memory from the 1950s ... unless you happened to be a girl! The additional editorial hook was the fact that in 1933 my grandfather had been awarded that Scouting Medal of Merit by Lord Baden Powell, so there was an element of history there as well as personal memories. This article would be just the thing for *Best of British,* but might also be of interest to *Scouting Magazine.*

The 2011 Royal Wedding of Prince William and Kate Middleton will have sparked off personal memories of other important events that involved the nation at a local level.

- The Coronation
- The Festival of Britain
- The Silver and Gold Jubilee
- The wedding of Diana Spencer and Prince Charles
- The wedding of Prince Charles and Camilla Parker-Bowles
- The Diamond Jubilee

We can remember quite clearly where we were on these occasions, with whom and how we took part in the celebrations. I missed local Coronation festivities because I had measles to match my white dress with scarlet spots on it ... but I did watch the Coronation ceremony live on a grainy black and white television at my grandparent's house. Some time later, pupils from our junior school were taken to the local cinema to watch the pageantry in full colour ... how do you remember that day?

The war years, the Rocking Fifties and the Swinging Sixties can evoke memories that we can say to other people *'Hey, do you remember ...?* Still one of my treasured possessions, I can recall reading my father's personal account of a desert battle, for the first time; and working my way through the complete *The War Illustrated* that my mother had collected for him to read when he came home – *he* never found the time. Listening to the CD collection *Dreamboats and Petticoats* conjuring up images of flared skirts with nipped-in waists and yards of net petticoat, dances at the village hall, coffee bars and music on the juke box. And they say if you can remember the Sixties, you weren't there! I can't say I remember much about the swinging bit, but I can recall Formula 1 racing, particularly at Silverstone; the Le Mans 24-hour race; holidays in France and jazz at The Stables.

These are some of *my* memories. Each one can be continuously re-packaged and re-labelled for selling to the different nostalgia magazines. Although we probably don't look upon ourselves as recorders of history, that is exactly what we are doing in keeping these memories alive via the pages of the nostalgia magazines. Because each one of these stories goes into the national archives with each publication – the University libraries of Aberystwyth, Cambridge, Dublin, Edinburgh, Oxford and the British Library – for posterity.

For example, an extract from my father's little notebook contains a snippet of WWII history, which has never been told. There's not enough technical detail for a full-length feature, which means it needs to be put into historical context, while at the same time having some contemporary significance. I went back to the original account, *With Pennants Flying* by David Masters, which was first published by Eyre & Spottiswoode in 1943; using this to set the scene for the diary I avoided the necessity of giving a lengthy introduction to the subject. A military magazine was interested in publishing the article but didn't want to pay ... so it appears here for the first time as an example of how to use a personal memoir, linked to both historical endorsement and the present.

A FORGOTTEN BATTLE OF THE DESERT CAMPAIGN – November 1941

In David Masters' well-known book about the Royal Armoured Corp, *With Pennants Flying,* there is a short chapter entitled 'The Last Stand', recording the 'unknown tank battle of Sheferzen' that took place in November 1941, during the Desert Campaign. Following the re-taking of the town of Sidi Omar from the Germans *'there were many Matilda tanks that had come to grief through minefield or gun to be gathered in by the Light Recovery Section ...'* These crippled tanks were gradually brought back to a wadi near Sheferzen, some ten miles from Sidi Omar. The wadi was concealed by a steep escarpment and became *'a hive of discreet industry with fitters wrestling with the Matilda tanks, which bore many an honoured battle-scar'.*

Some tanks were without tracks, others had turrets jammed by direct hits, others had faulty engines, or the hydraulics had been damaged. In order to carry out the repairs in the quickest possible time, it had been decided not to send the armour back to the main ordnance repair depot but to effect the repairs on the spot. On the morning of 25th November there were about eighteen crippled Matilda tanks in the wadi when the Germans attacked.

As David Masters writes: *'This unknown tank battle of Sheferzen*

... is one of the immortal stories of the Royal Armoured Corp' but there is another, until now, untold story of that fateful day of British soldiers who survived the murderous German onslaught. Cpl V H Parker [7630976] was serving with the 1st Army Tank Brigade, Light Recovery Section attached to the 42 and 44th Tank Regiments when he was caught up in what he always referred to as the battle of Sidi Omar. It is doubtful, until he read *With Pennants Flying* many years later, that he even knew the name of the wadi, which became a death trap for so many of his comrades.

The following is a verbatim account of his experience taken from his personal notebook that he carried at the time:

Sidi Omar 23-11-41
Heavy losses in tanks and infantry [Sussex], 12 tanks on the mines. The guns have been going all day, towards evening all is quiet. Flares dropping all round.
24-11-41
Tanks coming in for repairs, fighting going on about two miles away. Loads of Italian prisoners coming through, no Germans. Rather quiet this afternoon and evening again. There's something in the air – all day I have had a premonition of danger. Night draws on, the anti-tank gun is brought out and the Lewis gun – no one can sleep. I have disturbed Ernie a dozen times with my uneasiness. We are all told to stand by our rifles – the guard is doubled. Everyone is worried, for two days we have lost touch with Brigade. Machine guns are going to the south of us, this means Jerries behind and in front. Towards eleven a strong armour column is sighted in the moonlight going west up the escarpment.
25-11-41
The enemy have been located two miles south of the camp, a handful of us dig trenches and man the guns. About 11am a RASC truck comes dashing through – they have been chased

by armoured cars. They have been stopped on the south of the camp. We changed the gun pits to the west. The armoured cars are sighted on top of the escarpment; our officer sends a tank out but the cars clear off. We are absolutely surrounded. 12.15. We are told we are cut off from supplies. Thirty German tanks are heading south with 1000 guns and vehicles. We have five tanks in running order, the rest are under repair. 1.50pm. A long line of German tanks covering half the camp attack us – a non-combatant unit – from the east.

Our tanks engage the enemy, hell has broken loose, shells come over thicker than rain. It's a wonder anyone can live through it; we are caught in the crossfire. I have to find a deeper trench. I am as frightened as a child. I crawl to a slit trench, it's only about a foot deep and Jack Davies is in it. I lay on top of him and all this time prayers are coming out as one high explosive hits the parapet of the trench. I lay dazed and my head aches from the explosion – by this time I am passed caring. Sgt Magill [7599989 Sgt Magill W M] crawls on top of me. He lays exposed and I heard him say *"God bless us"* and then he was speaking to me; this helped me control my shattered nerves and I believe I would have run amok.

Gunner Gus lost his nerve and made a run for it, they opened up the machine guns then. I saw him throw up his hand and fall. He didn't move again. All this while I lay there, I waited for death to claim me. I expected them to go over us or gun us as we lay face down in the trench, by this time you couldn't lift your head.

Then through my dazed mind I heard, *"We are going to make a run for it."* Sgt Magill has gone and Davies is struggling for me to let him out. I look round – it is a scene of death and destruction. I decide to stop in the trench but I feel lonely on my own, I look out as Sgt Magill shouts: *"We are going"*. I can't face the machine guns and shells, twice I tried, and then I saw the motor move – and I saw it was then or never. With a prayer on my lips I ran the longest thirty yards I ever ran, and by an act of God I got there without a scratch. ASM Pope [7591475 ASM Pope E] was at the wheel with his foot down hard. Bullets were flying passed, shells burst to the right – he [the German gunner] had nearly got the range.

About two miles out we stopped to look back. The air was full of black smoke. We decided to head west but we were headed off by armoured cars - these chased us south. After getting away from them we were chased about three miles east by a light tank. This we easily left behind. About 5.30 we reached [?] We settled down for the night but no one slept. Out of nearly two hundred men, tanks and ordnance only seven of us got out.

26-11-41

Another day here and four of us haven't a thing, only what we wear. I have lost everything but my cigarette case with my dear wife's photo in, this never leaves me, my watch I left in my coat pocket. Can get no news of our camp only that Jerry is causing a trail of destruction, taking no prisoners – shooting everyone they capture. This stops us going north again.

27-11-41 Still no news

28-11-41 Still no news

29-11-41 The padre found us today. He tells us four of our lads are safe. One is my mate Ernie. I have been worried all the time about him.

30-11-41

We travel north-west about thirty miles. We pass German transport and tanks smashed up, Jerry's about shot his bolt. Towards evening we get to Brigade. I embraced Ernie – I could have kissed him for joy. I see burnt out lorries and tanks. Looking over the camp they are burying the dead. The RAF had blown the camp to bits, and then at night as the RAF do. One of the lads from our old camp had been killed. I lost a friend who walked into Cambridge Barracks the same day as myself – he was Bill Pearson of the LAD. At night on the news they say our AF have successfully bombed and destroyed enemy transport. A battle is raging over the hill and we are to move south till they have finished.

1-12-41

Had a shave today – first time for eleven days, washing and shaving being banned. We are living on bully and biscuits day in and day out, I won't be able to look a cow in the face after this.

2-12-41

Today we left for the old camp at 7.00am – no breakfast with the recovery. I couldn't recognise the place at all – battered tanks and lorries all over the place. All I could find of my kit was a scout photo, my sister's photo and my Part 2 pay book, which was a relief to me. We recovered three high tanks, one light, three lorries and our own machinery truck and trailer. We arrived back at dusk to a bit of bully and no tea.

5-12-41

Heard we are leaving for Tobruk this afternoon …

At the front of his notebook my father drew a memorial cross that contained the words: *In Memory of the boys of the LRS who fell at Sidi Omar 25-11-41*. He carried this notebook with him until the end of the war, and after serving with the 79th Armoured Division, going into France on Day +1, was eventually demobbed at Lüneberg in 1946. My mother's photograph mentioned in the diary also survived the war, and is part of the family grouping on the sitting room wall, together with a case containing my father's medals and his notebook.

The opening paragraph, containing that famous 'hook', tells us **when, where, why** and **what** was happening at the time of the account. It also provides a reference for those who may wish to find out more about the engagement, and the reason for including the army numbers of some of the soldiers involved. My father's account describes **how** it came to be written, and I resisted the urge to edit because I didn't want to destroy the essence of a narrative that had been written down as it occurred. He had many other brushes with death during the remainder of the war, but he always said this was the most terrifying – those crippled Matilda tanks fighting off the might of Rommel's armour, unable to move or manoeuvre until one by one they were knocked out. The poignant reference to my mother's photograph in the middle of all the chaos, provides the link with the present.

How many of our parent's and grandparent's stories have been lost because they were never written down and recorded? Old-fashioned sentimentality may no longer have a place in contemporary publishing, but there are always ways of presenting a piece of nostalgia that will appeal to an editor.

⇨ **It's just a matter of finding the right approach.**

Long-term Memory

Long-term memory can be thought of as referring to the more ancient past being re-visited in the present. This is not a dull description of Westminster Abbey with an architectural resume of the famous who have been crowned, married and buried there – but any editor would have welcomed a piece on the floral decorations for the Royal Wedding, especially if it included quotes from the florist, or the gardener who originally grew the trees. A visitor to the Abbey just after the event might have picked up on this and written a piece for a local magazine.

Here we can move away from the nostalgia market and focus on a much wider range of publications. Remember that nearly every county has a glossy magazine devoted to people, places, history, culture and culinary information specifically aimed at folk living in the region. The magazines are predominantly made up of advertisements placed by local traders, calendars of forth-coming events and photographs taken at important social events.

There are, however, usually two or three features on related topics, rather than articles of a general nature. Payment is negotiable but articles with an advertising slant, i.e. promoting a local business, are not usually paid for.

One of my favourites is *Coast & Country Living* which covers Mid and North Wales, Shropshire and Cheshire, and *Welsh Country Magazine,* which welcomes personal experience/ viewpoint pieces, historical or contemporary but there needs to be a strong Welsh connection. Each regional magazine has its own distinctive style, however, so it's essential to study them individually and not submit material on spec. Editors also tend to prefer material written by someone with a personal connection to that particular county or region. For example:

GONE PICKING ...1950's STYLE (*The Countryman*)
A summer harvest to be remembered comes from where gentle sea breezes blow inland from the English Channel across the orchards of Kent. The early morning sun has burned off the sea-fret that crept inland overnight, and overhead the sky is a bright burnished blue. It's the time for the annual cherry picking and it seems that almost by some mysterious telepathy, the Romany wagons begin arriving as they've done ever since we can remember – old lorries rubbing hubs with traditional horse-drawn painted caravans.

Kent has long been famous for its cherries, which have flourished there since Roman times. The wild cherry was listed by Aelfric (a Benedictine monk of Cerne Abbas) in his *Colloquy,* as a native of Britain but it is believed that the Romans introduced the cultivated variety, and that medieval monk-gardeners grafted more productive varieties onto the rootstock of the wild trees. In later times the fruit was taken to London to be sold in the city streets, where the cherry sellers cried their wares, and Samuel Pepys mentions buying cherries for his wife, in his famous *Diary* of the 1660s.

From the same period comes *Cherry Ripe,* a traditional English song with words by the poet Robert Herrick (1591-1674) - music added later by Charles Edward Horn (1786-1849) - which contains the well-known refrain of the cherry-sellers:

Cherry ripe, cherry ripe, Ripe I cry,
Full and fair ones Come and buy.
Cherry ripe, cherry ripe, Ripe I cry,
Full and fair ones Come and buy.

There is also an earlier poem by Thomas Campion (1567–1620) using the same title *Cherry Ripe,* which has other similarities and suggests that the sight of the cherry-sellers must have been a common one in the 17th century. The song became popular again during World War I, and in more recent years was heard in the 1982 film *Victor/Victoria,* sung by Julie Andrews at her character's unsuccessful audition at a nightclub. The fruit, bark and gum of the cherry trees were used to sooth irritating coughs, treat bronchial complaints and improve digestion. Crushed cherries, applied externally, were reputed to refresh tired skin and relieve migraines. According to the 17th century apothecary and physician, Thomas Culpeper, in his now famous *Complete Herbal,* the gum disolved in wine, *"is good for a cold, cough and harseness of the throat; mendeth the colour in the face, sharpeneth the eye-sight, provoketh appetite, and helpeth to break and expel the stone."*

In the kitchen, the fruit was cooked, eaten raw or (pulped with the stones) made into wine. It was also used to make conserves and liqueur. In medieval times cherries were picked when they were wine-red and eaten ultra-ripe but we're not thinking about our cherry-stained history as the flat wagons trundle out to the orchards with the fruit pickers on board. It doesn't matter in which direction we look, the cherry trees stand in regimented rows as far as the eye can see.

These sweet cherries grow on magnificent full-standard trees planted some 40ft apart, and the grass in between has been clipped short by grazing sheep. This is the most demanding of all fruit trees and can only be grown satisfactorily in the deep brick-earth soils largely found in Kent. Starlings and other fruit-eating birds flock from miles around, so cherries have to be grown in large enough numbers to justify various bird-scaring devices that the farmer has to employ as the fruit ripens.

Families are already out among the trees with baskets and the huge inverted V-shaped, wooden ladders to begin stripping the ripe fruit from among the sheltering leaves. Local families work shoulder to shoulder with Romany families; the women wearing brightly coloured headscarves as protection from the blistering rays from the sun. Our noses and shoulders carry the white smear of calamine lotion to sooth yesterday's sunburn, as we wait at the bottom of the ladder to tip cherries into the big baskets that will earn the family its day's wages. It's hard work but all around there is a pervading sense of camaraderie and laughter.

It's a long, hot afternoon ahead and we watch anxiously as the baskets seem a long way from being filled. The setting sun finally heralds the close of another day and it's almost dusk by the time we present our overflowing baskets for weighing. The Romany fires have been lit and mouth-watering smells follow us as we ride our bikes down the winding lane. Almost too tired to think about supper, we cycle home just as a sprinkling of stars begin appearing in the west. There's a contemporary Romany poem that just about sums up those memories:

"Fruit picking in the summer we always did in Kent,
In the cherry orchards was the best time that I've spent,
If I could go back in time, I know right where I'd be,
Sitting on a cherry box as my father played for me!"

Here's another example of historical detail being mingled with personal reminiscences. Again the opening lines set the scene of **what, when, where** and **why**, the narrator (in this case my partner) provides the **how**. I added the historical references and together we produced this piece for *The Countryman* and the Kent archive.

We tend to think of regional magazines as merely glossies with lots of colour photographs, reflecting a comfortable life-style, but there is another side to the publishing coin. *The Big Issue* was founded in 1991 and is described as an 'award-winning campaigning and street-wise general interest magazine'. The magazine covers London, the Midlands, the North East and South of England, with separate editions for Manchester, Scotland, Wales and the South West. Freelance submissions are welcome but each editor is looking for hard-hitting journalism pertinent to the region. They welcome interviews, campaign news, social comment and opinion, as well as arts and cultural features: the best approach is an emailed synopsis to the relevant editor but do read a couple of issues of the relevant magazine before submitting.

Regional newspapers (not the free papers) may also offer a marketplace, providing you have familiarised yourself with current editorial requirements, and probably have family connections to the area. Some of the papers have regular special sections that feature travel, children's pages, fashion and lifestyle, property, business and finance, cars, food, gardening and arts. Similar submissions would also be suitable for regional magazines, although, needless to say, any proposals would have to be relevant to the distribution area.

⇨ **Seasonal pieces would need to be submitted six or even twelve months in advance, as many of these magazines are quarterly. Seasonal or local recipes to accompany the article are always a good selling aid and, again, if your roots are go deep in that area, there may be a useful market for your writing.**

Is there a book in it?

If you have in-depth knowledge of your county's history, customs or folklore, it may also be worth looking at some of the independent publishers who produce a 'regional series' of books. These cover various topics from country pubs, ghostly happenings and grisly murders county by county.

One that immediately springs to mind is Shire Publications, and although you don't have to live in the relevant county to write books for them, it does help.

Most Shire titles are part of a series: 'Discovering' books are non-fiction paperbacks of varying lengths on subjects as diverse as *Discovering Ipswich, Discovering Buckinghamshire, Discovering English Fairs, Discovering Battlefields of Southern England, Discovering Lost Theatres,* etc. Apart from the 'Discovering' titles, there are also series covering Shire Albums, History in Camera, Shire Archaeology, Shire County Guides, Shire Natural History, Shire Garden Guides and Gothick Guides and as owner, John Rotheroe says: *"Shire specialises in small books on all manner of obscure subjects."* And although more recent tiles like *Church Fonts, Haunted Inns* and *Discovering Preserved Railways* have a very distinct rural feel, check out the website and see if you have any ideas that would produce a 'small book' for this publisher.

When travelling around the country on business or holiday, study the 'local interest' publications that are available in small bookshops and libraries, and make a note of the publisher's address. Take a couple of samples with you as a guide to the house-style and when you get home, write your proposal. Do bear in mind, however, that many of these little books are self-published and often make a tidy profit for the author, selling through local gift shops and post offices where tourists are likely to buy them.

Many of those writers who choose to go down the self-publishing route *are* still interested in earning money from their efforts. Publishing is evolving all the time although it's a rare self-published book that manages to make its author a fortune, simply because it is usually catering for a niche market and there is always the problem of selling the thing once you've got it home! It is now even more important for an author to be fully conversant with the on-line market place, in addition to the old faithfulls who appear annually in the writers' handbooks.

A writer doesn't need to self-publish unless the book is so specialised that only a handful are likely to sell to those with a similar interest. Often these specialist publications are the only way of preserving information for posterity and the authors *do* make a valuable contribution to publishing history. There is no stigma attached to this particular area of self-publishing, simply because of the limited interest as far as a main-stream publishing houses are concerned in local history. The main problem with self publication is distribution, but if you have a ready-made outlet on your doorstep through tourist sales, then it is something to be considered - and will only add to your portfolio if the book is professionally presented.

⇨ **There are always other outlets and options**

Handy Hint:
Trawl the internet and *Willings Press Guide* for submission guidelines for all publishers specialising in nostalgia – especially those that cater for overseas readers. Keep the guidelines for those that look like hopefuls on your computer for handy reference, and study the layout and approach for titles on their back-list. When you feel you have enough material for each subject area, send a proposal to the most likely publisher, together with the full chapter breakdown and a c.v.

Try This Exercise:

We all have old photographs tucked away in drawers and boxes that spark off family memories and stories of the past. Make a selection of six of these yellowing photos and study each one carefully for ideas for a contemporary short story, poem or article that might suit one of the publications mentioned in this chapter.

- Or perhaps it would be better targeted as a competition entry where your imagination can have free-rein.

Chapter Eighteen

Memory Lane

"Took the dogs to the woods yesterday and the bluebells are out; the perfume and the rippling blue haze was absolutely gorgeous. I love the woods; they still hold that scary, unpredictable magic feeling. What might be lurking behind the next tree? The movement of the branches causing a flickering dappled sunshine effect. All in the imagination ... until in the silence a pheasant suddenly goes up and you nearly pooh your pants!" **Extract from a letter from a childhood friend.**

It is said that the past is another country, and if this is so, then it is a journey we can make with the minimum of preparation but with the maximum amount of enjoyment. Those 'things that arouse fond memories of the past' can often be used as cameos in our writing in the same ways as we discussed family resources in an earlier chapter.

The five 'things' I'd chosen: a collection of old family photographs, old theatre programmes, a particular piece of music, wood smoke, and the smell of hawthorn or bluebells in blossom are fairly obvious choices but even those who share some of our memories will have a different mind-picture of events or places. For example, a favourite childhood haunt was a place called the Quarries that was used by our local Scout troupe for their summer camp. My main memory of the Quarries is of the masses of hawthorn trees in bloom ... my friend's spontaneous memory is of a rather unpredictable horse that used to come charging through the trees and frighten us to death. Now I hadn't forgotten the horse but it wasn't *the* thing that triggers my memory – as it happens, my friend doesn't recall the hawthorn!

We both have vivid memories of those bluebells at Shrob Lodge.

Now remember your childhood places. Can you see them … or better still, can you *use* them? I've already mentioned my use of the local woods as being the setting for *Whittlewood*, and I'm currently using the old wharf at Old Stratford (where the barges used to turn on their way along the Buckingham Arm) in another novel in progress, *The Waterboatman*. Like the old forest, this part of the canal is long gone and survives only a childhood memory but, by using the right-brain zip-files, I can re-create this towpath vividly whenever I need to call on it for inclusion in the text.

Setting the Scene

Our ability to write a good story from childhood memories doesn't, however, confine us to virtual-reality. The memories may stir up ideas from childhood but we don't have to use them in that same context, i.e. through the eyes of a child. For example:

A few years ago, I attended a Welsh Game Fair with a group of friends. In the main arena, one of the attractions was a chap who was simulating all the old poacher's tricks for the entertainment of the crowd. His display was cleverly contrived by using a series of elastic lures to make the fake 'rabbits' streak across the field into the long-net. It was so convincing that two visiting whippets joined in the fun, much to the delight of the crowd and the embarrassment of the owner.

I'd been watching the display with a view to writing an article about it but instead of taking in the details of the here and now, my subconscious mind was re-living my own memories of poaching that had been long forgotten. Like Faust's *madeleines*, it was the running of the long-net that triggered the memory. A long-net was some two foot high and some 20 feet long, and held up right by cut hazel sticks … how did I know they were hazel sticks? Because it had been my job to carry them

The story goes back to my pre-school years and my father left baby-sitting for reasons I can't now remember. He'd done the

1940-45 stint in North Africa and Europe and it took a long, long time to get the need for an adrenalin buzz out of his system. Being a countryman, he turned his hand to a spot of DIY recreational therapy (i.e. poaching) because that was the way you coped in those pre-counselling days. It was a fine night with a poacher's moon; myself (aged about four) and the dog (about the same age) were bundled onto the motorbike and off we went into the darkness of the woods for a few hours of illegal hunting.

This happened several times until my mother found out – then there was all hell to pay and my night-time excursions were stopped. Today, social services would consider leaving a four-year old alone in the dark holding a poacher's net, the act of extreme neglect, if not cruelty. For me, it represents ultimate trust in the person closest to me. The long-term effect is that I have no fear of being alone in remote places during the hours of darkness – which was just as well when I lived in Wales and used to roam about the fields at midnight with the dog, star-watching. Or where we live now in the Galtee Mountains.

I've included this tale because I've told it (and similar) so many times at writers' workshops as an illustration of how the strangest and most unexpected things can trigger a useful memory. It gives the extra personal touch to what may otherwise be a straight forward report of a country fair; it bridges then and now with the added bonus of human interest, which is an essential ingredient when writing for mainstream editors.

➪ **If we write about the past in terms of nostalgia, the market is limited; if we use bridging-techniques it gives added dimension.**

A Flash of Brilliant Colour

Let's see what else a good rummage in the right-brain zip-files can produce ... after all, family photographs, old theatre programmes, music, wood smoke, the smell of flowers are pretty clichéd, aren't they? Let's implement the mapping technique and see where these ideas lead …

What about an indelible memory of Stonehenge? We've all been there, seen the summer solstice celebrations on television, and marvelled at the wonder of Neolithic engineering, so what else can be said about it? I can vividly recall visiting the ancient monument as the sun was rising on the winter solstice and there wasn't another soul about in those pre-fenced off days. There was a heavy hoare-frost that morning and looking out over the Plain the world was enveloped in an eerie, silver silence. On the distant horizon, the sun was a bright red orb in a smokey-blue haze, causing the frost on the upright stones to shimmer like running water as the blood-red light reflected on the ice. As the sunlight intensified, the smokey colours evaporated and somewhere a bird began to sing - the spell was broken. And I have never wanted to visit Stonehenge again because nothing can ever compare to that wonderful, one-off Otherworld experience.

Old theatre programmes remind me of *Napoleon,* an epic silent French film directed by Abel Gance, telling the story of the rise of the French Emperor, beginning as a youth in school where he managed a snowball fight like a military campaign, to his victory in invading Italy in 1797. Planned to be the first of six movies about Napoleon Bonaparte, it was first released in a gala premiere at the Paris Opéra in April 1927. Film historian Kevin Brownlow began the reconstruction in the years leading up to 1980, having purchased two 9.5mm reels of the film from a street market, which led to a lifelong fascination with the film and a quest to reconstruct it. Further restoration was in 1983 and again in 2000, including footage rediscovered by the Cinémathèque Française. The film is screened in full restoration very rarely due to the difficult requirement of three projectors for the Polyvision section. The 1983 screening of the film at the Barbican Centre in London (where I saw this piece of cinema history) included a live orchestral score of pastiche classical music arranged and conducted by Carl Davis. A wonderful evening.

A never to be repeated musical interlude took place at Beverly Minster while I was visiting a friend in the area. The Minster itself is an imposing architectural marvel, founded on the site of an original Saxon church dating back to 8th century. Classed as one of the masterpieces of medieval art, the Minster was being prepared for a classical concert later that evening, and as we sat looking up at the magnificent vaulting, my friend began to sing in plain-song. As her beautiful voice filled nave and transept, people stopped to listen as the perfect acoustics carried the notes to every corner of the church. It still sends shivers down my spine when I remember it.

It's probably not often that slate mines can produce the tingle-factor in the memory but the disused quarry at Abereiddy, a hamlet in Pembrokeshire, always manages to create that feeling. Hidden along a narrow, twisting lane with high banks on either side is the ruin of a small group of houses known as The Street. These were houses built for the quarry workers and were still occupied until the 1930s when the combination of a violent storm that caused disastrous flooding and an outbreak of typhoid led to their abandonment. Up over the cliff from the beach is what is now known as the Blue Lagoon, the large quarry, now filled with seawater through a breach in the outer wall. Despite the name, the water is always a distinct turquoise-greenish colour, due to the mineral content within the quarry. The lagoon is now a favourite place for adventure groups but when we first discovered it, it was a magical place, filled with a raw beauty of its own. I still have a large piece of slate from there, worn smooth by the tides, that I use as a bird table here in Ireland – perhaps it's because we're both a long way from home that it's a constant reminder of that lovely windswept beach and the clear blue pool.

None of these trips down memory lane, however, have any literary significance whatsoever. They are merely little cameos of memory that aren't important or big enough to warrant a piece about them, even though they're all related to some historical occurrence. In truth I haven't thought about them for a long time but in waking up the right-brain for the purpose of this book, they suddenly appeared in a flash of brilliant colour, as vivid and crystal-clear as the first time. At some later date I will probably use them in a new piece of writing because I have a ready-made scenario stored away in my right-brain zip-file. In fact, the bluebell wood and the wood smoke have already found a place in a new book …

It wasn't always blue skies

So far we've indulged ourselves in all the good things from our childhood days but using the mapping techniques, let's turn a child's (or teenager's) world upside down and try to remember some of the not so good things. It's not so easy as it sounds. Because the brain has this remarkable function of burying unpleasantness, it is much more difficult to recall the darker elements of childhood – but this is where a writer's heart must dwell. Powerful writing needs to contain these darker elements, so let's see what I can come up with on this level and recall five things that could be developed:

- During my lifetime I've been bitten by dogs more times than I can recall. The first was as a three-year old jumping on the dog kennel while the dog was eating bone (I'd been told to keep away), and the last was a year ago when I was bitten in the face by a wolfhound-cross (wearing glasses at the time saved me from really serious damage). For all the damage, it's never put me off dogs and I currently have seven greyhounds of my own - but from the writer's point of view there are all sorts of possibilities for developing character background.

- Possibly the nearest I ever came to death was going through the ice when the canal froze over. Fortunately for me I had the loop of the dog's lead around my wrist and she stopped me from going under. I remember being more scared of going home with wet clothes than admitting I'd been on the ice. The dog, Sadie, incidentally, was the same one who bit me for jumping on the kennel, and my partner in poaching! How could a writer use this type of memory … in a short story perhaps?

- Another potential dark day was discovering my dog was missing. This one (Kelpie) was a Jack Russell I'd had as a puppy and we went everywhere together. I walked for miles around the fields calling until at last I heard a muffled response. She'd been caught in an old rabbit snare and luckily the buckle on her collar had prevented her from choking during the hours she'd been missing. I ripped out every snare I could find and weighed with a large stone, they were dropped in the deepest part of the river. I thing I remember most vividly is the black rage I felt rather than relief.

- An instance with people involvement happened during a school holiday to Switzerland, on a day-trip to Lucern. My classmates thought it would be amusing to leave me alone in the strange town, and hid while I tried to find them. As it happened they lost sight of me and spent an anxious few hours trying to pick up *my* trail. In the meantime, I went sight-seeing alone and found some amazing places before it was time to meet up at a pre-arranged lunch venue. Their plan had backfired but I was still extremely upset at the cruel trick they'd played.

- I've already mentioned Coronation Day when I sat at home with measles while all my friends partied on the local recreational ground. I'd had a special dress for the occasion - white muslin with tiny embroidered scarlet spots – and wore it to watch the ceremony on television. Perhaps my mother thought that getting dressed up would make me feel better – but it didn't. And I never wore the dress again. I can never see shots from the Coronation on television without remembering missing out on the celebrations.

Now those five instances took a lot longer to recall than the good things in life, but it demonstrates how we can dig deep down into our subconscious and come up with old memories that we'd thought were forgotten. These are the instances we use for explaining why a character reacts to a given set of circumstances in the way they do …

⇨ **Try to remember five 'dark days' of your own and record them in your Ideas Book for possible future use.**

Memories in the making

If we choose to record our actions and thoughts for posterity along more ambitious lines, we may produce something along the lines of Peter Mayle's *A Year in Provence,* which captivated the imagination of television audiences for weeks in 1993 via the superb acting performance of John Thaw. Originally published in 1989, *A Year in Provence* became an international bestseller that chronicled a year of the author's life as a British expatriate in Ménerbes, a village in the southern *département* Vaucluse.

The book is actually a light-hearted autobiography in addition to being a travel and restaurant guide, and a cultural study of the south of France. As one reviewer wrote, Mayle recounts a year of their adventures living and working amid the

French, the nosiness of neighbours who are the self-proclaimed experts on everything from geophysics to truffle hunting, French bureaucracy, and the hordes of rude tourists. The television series added the glamour and together, Mayle and Thaw produced a heady cocktail of exotic location, glamour, humour, dreamscape and an appealing cast of amiable foreigners that sent thousands of holiday-makers and potential ex-pats scurrying for a taste of southern France. In fact, the British Book Awards named *A Year in Provence* Best Travel Book of the Year (1989) and Peter Mayle Author of the Year in 1992; the French government made him a *Chevalier de la Légion d'honneur* (Knight of the Legion of Honor) in 2002, for *coopération et francophonie*.

Now, some 20 years later, Michael Wright's *C'est La Folie* and *Je t'aime á La Folie* gives us a more domestic approach to living in the rural heartlands of France. This former theatre critic and literary diarist chronicled his move to France in a regular column in the *Daily Telegraph* before turning his hand to becoming an author. His adventures and misunderstandings with the locals (not to mention his sheep and chickens) have a much more domestic and romantic approach as Wright progresses from rustic hermit to farmer *en famille*.

These successes have me toying with the idea of trying something similar with The Glen because even the short move across St George's Channel throws up all sorts of cultural differences, especially for a non-Catholic in a stanch Catholic community – which in itself creates all manner of humorous situations. Nevertheless, as we observed in *Signposts For Country Living*, we do know a thing or two about integrating into rural communities, and as long as we can talk about 'dogs and horses', it gives us a head start over other in-comers who have come purely for the view! *Signposts* itself was based on memories taken from other locations in England and Wales and acquired over the years, from childhood up to the present day.

➪ **The more we unzip the memories and experiences that are stored away in the right-brain, the easier it becomes to access them until we can do it at will. To use Laurie Lee's analogy, we stumble on a form of writing that sets off these recollections and we quickly learn to utilise them.**

Handy Hint:
Open up a 'clippings' file to contain anything that reminds you of your past. Have a sort through every six months and discard anything that now draws a blank; keep anything that still triggers a memory, no matter how small, for possible use in the future. The bulk of my clippings file is made up of material sent by a friend who still lives in our home town, and who cuts out anything she thinks may be of interest from the local weekly paper.

Try This Exercise:
Select a 'common theme' from any one of the childhood-related 'things' listed in your Ideas Book and, using the bridging-technique, write about it from a different perspective, or in a different style, that you think would appeal to a mainstream editor.

- This can be in the form of a short story, article or poem but it needs to link the past with something that is pertinent for today.

Chapter Nineteen

A Novel Idea

"There was never a good biography of a good novelist. There couldn't be. He is too many people if he's any good." **F Scott Fitzgerald**

Sooner or later the writer will decide that the time is right to start writing a novel, but there are a few things we need to take into account before we start. If we've served our apprenticeship well, we will have learned all the tricks of the trade when it comes to making every word count.

- Non-fiction writing will have taught us how to stimulate the imagination in our readers and economy of language. Which is why experienced journalists often make the best novelists.

- Short stories teach us not to waste time on lengthy description and superfluous dialogue.

- Poetry shows us how to create powerful images with the minimum amount of words.

We appreciate the importance of conflict, people-pictures and human-interest to stir the emotions and make the reader want to find out more about the characters we have created. We know that personal experiences can be re-moulded to fit other circumstances and because they are personal to ourselves, we can write about them passionately and with some conviction.

Opening Gambit

It's been said that the most difficult thing we ever write is the opening line of our first book. But even if you can't think of a punchy, riveting, gut-churning first line, press on with your narrative – or at least carry on preparing the framework of the story. On a personal note, I find it impossible to make a serious start on a book until the first line has been carefully honed and perfected to my complete satisfaction. The sudden appearance of the first line is my sign to say that I'm ready to get down to the serious business of writing.

Nevertheless, there aren't any hard and fast rules over what makes a great opening but unless a publisher or agent is caught by it, there will be little chance of him reading further. The opening needs to have impact; to reach out and seize you by the throat; smack you between the eyes; punch you in the gut.

Good openings set a scene or period by evoking time and place, like the start of Grace Metalious's *Return to Peyton Place*:

> *"Sometimes, winter comes gradually to northern New England so that there is an element of order and sequence to time and season, and when the first snow comes it is not surprising because it has been expected for quite a while."*

Or introduce a character as in Graham Greene's *Travels With My Aunt*:

> *"I met my Aunt Augusta for the first time in more than half a century at my mother's funeral."*

Or reveal the immediate problem or drama as in Stella Gibbon's *Cold Comfort Farm*:

> *"The education bestowed on Flora Poste by her parents had been too expensive, athletic and prolonged; and when they died within a few*

> *weeks of one another during the annual epidemic of the influenza or Spanish Plague which occurred in her twentieth year, she was discovered to possess every art and grace save that of earning her own living."*

Most serious writers will admit to being avaricious readers in their childhood. Nine times out of ten it was the ability to empathise with a favourite author's creativity and enjoy the shared escapism that triggered the desire to become a writer in later life. This subconscious store of favourite titles can also provide the stimulus for creative impulses when we come to plot our own novels.

Using the basic theme or plot from a classic source has been described as 'metatext'. This does not mean that we are plagiarising the original author's ideas, we are merely pushing the original concept into another dimension. For example, the idea of Daphne du Maurier's *Rebecca* creates the dramatic scenario of the dead ruling the narrative from beyond the grave. This treatment would be accepted and acceptable in the horror genre but it can come as a bit of a surprise in romantic fiction.

As we know, Rebecca is already dead when we join the story but – love her or hate her – she is still a force to be reckoned with, even though we never 'see' her. This does not mean we will be driven to create another Manderley, or a similar cast of characters like Mrs Danvers and the de Winters. What we can do is transport the basic concept into another time and place so that the new story bears absolutely no resemblance to the original. Although parts of Rebecca are down-right creepy, du Maurier avoids any supernatural tricks – it is the sheer force of Rebecca's personality that creates the drama/conflict, not any ghostly happenings. The focus, however, doesn't need to be a dead wife, it can be any other member of the family, or a lover.

Crafting a Novel: Bones & Padding

All forms of writing start with a germ of an idea that slowly develops into something tangible and solid. More often than not, the idea has been germinating in the back of our minds for years; characters which have been slowly aiding the development of the dialogue and plot, not clamour to be heard aloud. But there is a vast gulf between starting a full-length book and finishing it. In an article in the American *Writers' Digest*, author C. Story points out: *"There's a talent part of writing and then there's the craft – and they're two different things. The talent comes in while conceptualising a story; the craft is what lets you put it on paper in a coherent form."*

The Bones

So we let our talent take care of the characterisation and plot. The following three exercises are the bare bones of starting to write your novel.

- In a card index system, large notebook or computer, set down the sequence of the story. The important thing is to have a clearly defined idea of where your story is going right from the start. There will be many crossroads and U-turns along the way, even the odd dead-end, but this is all part of learning the author's craft. The important thing is to get all those messy notes and unrelated ideas out of your head and into some semblance of manageable order either on paper or screen.

- Define your principal characters using the same system. Describe their characteristics, personality defects, virtues, colouring, quirks and foibles. The basis for your story is knowing in advance what is eventually going to happen to them.

- Prepare an outline of the complete novel. You need to decide on a starting point – past, present or future - that will effectively and believably link up with the conclusion. Trying to make it up as you go along doesn't work; you need to have a rough outline of when the events in the story are going to occur and in what sequence.

You may have your ending clearly mapped out but find at some later stage that the story has a different idea to the one in your outline. Don't be too hasty to disregard the messages because the unscheduled conclusion may turn out to be a more striking ending than the one you intended. 'Gut reaction' can be an important writer's aid – a side shoot of talent that should be carefully nurtured – so be prepared to take a risk.

An additional exercise in craftsmanship at this stage could also save hours of frustration once the book is finished. Trying to decide how long the typescript is going to be is a bit like asking: How long is a serpent's tail? But it is an important consideration in modern publishing. A boring thought, I agree, but it could save considerable effort at the end when you're trying to cut or stretch your typescript to fit the publisher's requirements. On the plus side, by having this information in advance does mean that you have a clearly defined framework within which to work, right from the start.

Once you have a chapter outline, details of your characters pinned up in front of you, and a broad synopsis of where the story is going to lead. Don't worry if you haven't thought of a catchy title – the idea will come out of the blue, and the last thing you want to waste time over at this stage, it what you are going to call it, since either you, or the publisher, will probably change it anyway. Let the characters tell their own stories (where possible) through dialogue and action, whilst avoiding pages of high-blown prose – today's publishers don't like it. And don't feel compelled to include every single detail about your location, characters and plot in the first chapter. You'll overload your reader with detail when what they want is action.

By using your chapter outline and synopsis it will be easier for you to keep track of the events shaping the plot. If you have room, use spread sheets pinned up on a board, and if you can't remember when the hero first confessed his impotence, a quick glance at our charts will put you back in gear without the need to flick back through dozens of pages.

Conflict and Drama as Part of the Plot

When we decide to begin writing a novel, it's probably the idea of conflict and drama that prompts us to begin. These ingredients are as important as characterisation and essential to the plot. Conflict and drama presents the series of difficulties that prevent problems within the plot from being resolved, or our characters from achieving their goal. Conflict is the barrier between opposing ideas, characters or events that create the drama within the story, and is integral to the development of the plot. To achieve this, we should:

- Start with a 'hook' that will intrigue the reader right from the start and draw them into the story. Therefore our beginning should be a moment of drama or surprise. Background details can come later.

- Structure the chapters to provide a equal balance of peaks and troughs to give our story a variety of pace by interweaving sections of high drama with gentler, more reflective scenes. If necessary, cut longer scenes into two and insert another scene in another location featuring different characters. This technique allows us to introduce another thread to the plot, and at the same time keep the reader guessing, just as they do in a script for a television series.

- Build drama gradually as it would develop in life but employ cliff-hangers at the end of each chapters. It may be a well-used technique but it still works as we can see from its constant use in television soaps. Cliff-hangers do not have to be overly dramatic just so long as they pose some sort of question or unresolved situation that will make readers want to read on.

- Subtly introduce clues to what will happen in the future to avoid the conclusion seeming illogical and unsatisfactory. Unpredictability and surprise are valuable tools up the writer's sleeve, but they will only work as long as enough clues have been laid.

- Create changes in atmosphere through description, thoughts and dialogue. This is a subtle way of creating a sense of tension, or lulling the reader into a false sense of security.

Conflict and Drama Through Characters

As we discussed in Chapter Ten: *Dramatis Personae,* when we create characters these will be the instruments of creating conflict and drama within the plot. We cannot go from beginning to end without some crisis developing to provide tension or animosity between them. To achieve this we should:

- Give our protagonists different values, backgrounds, aims and ambitions, etc., we are creating contrasts - and such contrasts are likely to result in conflict and drama to drive the story along.

- Introduce inner turmoil whether it is a hidden fear or a difficult decision that has to be made, or conflicting loyalties. This is also important to the development of the story. Most of us have experienced problems during our lives, and the inner conflict revealed through character viewpoint, should be designed to engage reader empathy. If the reader cares about the characters, they will want to find out how the problems are going to be resolved.

- Not create characters that are always passive or victims; they should be allowed to change and mature during the story. This is all part of the development of the plot.

Conflict and Drama Due to Events

The sequence of events during a novel should automatically create the elements of drama, tension and conflict that were given earlier in the Polti Theory. We should strive to:

- Create tension through circumstances because something needs to happen to a character to develop the storyline. Circumstances should create the drama.

- Create conflict or drama because of a misunderstanding: a technique is often used in romantic fiction. If we are to introduce a hero at the start of the story and yet stop him from getting it together with our heroine until the end of the story, there's got to be a good reason — or more usually a series of reasons. Misunderstandings and misinterpretation of situations, dialogue are useful devices - so long as they remain credible.

Whatever the genre or theme, conflict and drama are indispensable elements of novel writing. Using them skilfully means we can keep our readers interested, our characters fired up and ready for action, and our narrative fresh, exciting and full of 'the X-factor'.

The Padding

Padding in a novel should not be confused with page-filling wordage. Very often there are pages of description and dialogue that do not serve any purpose other than to help the novel reach the minimum word count required by the publisher. The padding is the ***technique*** used to flesh out the bones of the novel, and to create the right setting in which to tell the story.

Whether the novel we are writing is character driven or plot driven, whether we are writing crime, literary fiction, science fiction, fantasy or any other genre, the setting we choose is also an integral part of our novel. This is because setting provides a backdrop against which our characters will be enacting their drama. The setting provides a visual picture for our readers of Georgian England, the planet Titan, or the French Riviera - and adds authenticity. Without a convincing setting, our plot and our characters would exist in a vacuum. So where do we begin?

Selecting a period in history

If we choose to write period fiction (and remember even the 1960s are classed as history now), we should.

- **Research the period thoroughly.** There is no excuse for inaccurate information. By the time we are finished, we need to be living and breathing the period so that it takes little effort for us to write about it convincingly.

- Remember that **the best research is unobtrusive** in the finished story. It should not be obvious, and what is left out may be just as important as what is left in. Too much detail will stifle the fictional qualities of the novel.

- Use **research to fuel motivation and plot.** This is a chance to let our imagination go to work and possibly use real characters, or events to flesh out the story.

Setting the time span

We also need to decide when our story will begin and when it will end. A novel doesn't need to go through the motions from cradle to grave, and often the most effective devices are not necessarily the obvious ones. We should

- **Begin at a point of interest or drama.** The reader must be drawn into our story from the first page, so there needs to be a hook. Any necessary background information leading up to this point of beginning can be given to the reader later in the story through dialogue, character introspection or flashback. That way, it won't clutter up the tension of our beginning.

- **Consider genre and plot.** Some genres (thrillers or murder mysteries) tend to use shorter time spans, because the emphasis is on plot; other genres (sagas, 'relationship' novels) often use a longer time span because they are character driven and therefore background, psychology, defiance and discord between the generations may be more important.

- Remember that a **short time span** means we need to have a lot happening in a short space of time. A **longer time span** requires careful representation of time passing without taking great leaps through time and space to move things along.

- **End as soon as possible after the dramatic climax or resolution** of the novel, even if it's open-ended. Further irrelevant action will spoil the structure of the story and dilute the impact of the ending. End with a bang not a whimper.

Choosing the right place

Before selecting a setting for our action to take place in, we need to think about developing in our reader's mind a sense of time and place. Do we know enough about a real place to write about it, or are we going to create a parallel world of our own imagination? We need to:

- Consider what we want our setting to achieve. Imagine the action taking place with different moods and atmosphere in an isolated village, a bleak moor, a city landscape, or a seaside town...

- Check that the setting will complement the other elements of the story. Does the plot require a lot of different people to be together in one place for a certain period of time? (Agatha Christie can still tell us a lot about that one). Can the setting be used to create tension, conflict, or even a theme for our story, as Mary Wesley's *Camomile Lawn* symbolised childhood, innocence and dreams?

- Think about using symbolism as we discussed in the Secrets Steps Nine and Ten, because a symbolic setting can add mood and layers of meaning. A place that held childhood memories for a character may have added significance for the adult; a bleak landscape can echo feelings of loneliness and vulnerability; a station platform may represent a journey of a different kind. Symbolism can add strength and depth to a story.

- If writing about a real place, remember that tourist offices are helpful, books and the Internet are invaluable, but nothing can replace absorbing the place in person, armed with camera and notebook. Our factual information must be scrupulously correct because if a reader should spot an inconsistency, they will to lose belief in our story - and may be compelled to write and tell us about it too!

- Consider creating a fictional town in a real county. This eliminates the risk of inaccuracy, allows us to create whatever our plot may require, and gives us the added bonus of a regional novel - we can use the actual surrounding countryside and regional atmosphere as part of our story. Giving our town a fictional name that is regionally accurate adds authenticity. Jilly Cooper is very good at using this technique.

- Draw sketches or maps of interiors, houses, towns, etc., as part of the planning process. This will help us be consistent with our descriptions and enable us to visualise the environment ourselves. It is easy to forget which way a character should turn when he leaves his house to go to the river, or whether his sitting room has a couch, or how many armchairs. Continuity is vital to retain authenticity.

- Connect characters with their environment by using viewpoint. When we describe a place it becomes more interesting, more individual and more relevant if it is described through the eyes of one of our characters. It adds the emotions, mood and thoughts of that character, while developing characterisation at the same time.

- Avoid large chunks of background description. Description of the setting is more effective when interwoven with dialogue, action and introspection, so that the reader gets a feel for the place without getting description indigestion. Balzac's epic descriptions would never be found in the contemporary novel.

- Make settings authentic by using (where appropriate) local industry, dress and regional customs, lifestyle including food, architecture, transport, street life, local flora and fauna, and local weather conditions. It's these simple touches that create a sense of reality, thereby allowing the reader to suspend disbelief and become immersed in the story.

- Lengthy description of the setting may not be as important as it was in 19th-century literature, but without a certain amount of good, concise description, our characters would have nowhere to live and no time to live in.

What's Gone Wrong?

Writing the first draft of a book is the easy part. You've off-loaded all the ideas and got the characters all going in the right direction; there have been a few unexpected developments but nothing you couldn't handle – but it doesn't work. There's something missing.

These flaws probably manifest in what we have referred to as 'the padding'. As we've seen, this is the element of the novel that should add depth and dimension to the story. This doesn't mean that pages of description can be added to cure it; the solution is far subtler than that. Firstly, look at the characters you've created.

- Are they real enough for the reader to empathise with their traumas and difficulties; their lives and loves?

- Have you put too much emphasis on A's background, so that it becomes a total cop-out for decent feeling?

- Why are you, the author, justifying B's reaction to C, when you condemn D for a similar mistake?

- Is your story believable?

Which brings us to the plot:

- Have you explored everyone's motives?

- Nobody does anything without a reason, valid or not, so is there sufficient explanation for X's behaviour to Y?

- Or does it sound hollow and contrived?

Do *you* really care what happens to them? Because if you don't, how can you expect the reader to feel anything other than indifference? It is characterisation that moves the plot along and gets the reader believing in the story; if it's not working then it's back to the drawing board I'm afraid.

Long, physical descriptions also need careful pruning. If you feel characters have enough padding on their bones to make them real and compelling, what about the location? Again, pages of descriptive prose will not necessarily give the right atmosphere to draw the reader into the story. Lists of flora and fauna do not a novel make.

Also to be avoided is a Pickford's removal inventory of house contents. Again, you cannot create atmosphere from a furnishings or arts catalogue; neither does estate agent's parlance pass for good scene setting. *Atmosphere* is the key word when it comes to location. If you can't see your location, how can you expect your reader to? Unless you're familiar with your subject, make sure you have sufficient reference books to hand to fill in the gaps; or take yourself off for a weekend's break to somewhere similar to what you have in mind. There may be other things to consider:

- Are you trying to make some form of political or social statement that is insufficiently researched and therefore doesn't ring true?

- Have you cast your characters in a setting that lacks conviction because it is unfamiliar to you?

- Are you trying to be too clever for your own good?

These are, or course, hypothetical problems, but every first novel is subject to some (if not all) of them and every author who has ever written a novel has made the same errors in the early stages of their career, so you should not be afraid to admit yours.

Ambiguous endings

In that old Hollywood classic, *Now Voyager*, Bette Davies's famous words to her married lover are: *"Don't let's ask for the moon. We have the stars."* An innocuous enough little romantic phase that appears in countless books of cinematic quotations, but what does it mean?

On one hand, and that which probably came into the mind of the scriptwriter, was why strive for the unattainable when you can settle for a reasonably acceptable alternative. On the other, and the thought that would probably occur to the mystic, it could also mean why settle for the familiar and safe when you can reach out to infinity. Which would be your interpretation?

Different genres require different types of ending. When we type 'The End' of our novel, we have either dotted all the i's and crossed all the t's, or we have left a sense of mystery or continuance in the air. Romantic fiction usually requires a conclusive ending where everyone lives happily ever after in a cloud of tulle and antique lace – **and this is what the readers' want.** Your novel is their form of escapism, and woe betide the author who doesn't come up with the orange blossom and horse-drawn-carriage at the end.

Other genres are more demanding and often finish with a

sense of 'to be continued' even if the author has no intention of writing a sequel. This is probably what is meant by the saying that every novel remains unfinished until it is taken up by its readers. Even though the story has come to a satisfactory conclusion we, the reader, can add our own ideas about what is going to happen next – with the vague hope that we will meet the character(s) again. And yet how many times have we read a sequel that has been published due to popular demand and been bitterly disappointed?

Writing a novel is not an easy task; it's hard work, time consuming and, at times heartbreaking but the thing that will always separate the amateur from the serious writer, it that the serious writer will finish the job. And having finished it, will re-assess it, re-write it where necessary and continue to learn from the mistakes. The serious writer accepts that the first completion is, in effect, only the first draft. Before they considers it good enough to send to a publisher, the author will probably have re-written parts of the text several times before feeling completely happy with it.

⇨ **Have you got that kind of stamina?**
⇨ **If not, leave novel writing alone until you have.**

Handy Hints:
Keep a note of any great opening lines and try to write the first paragraph of a novel or short story. Or use them as a beginning for a piece of writing of your own and in a completely different genre. How about: *"It was the best of times; it was the worst of times ..."* the famous opening line from Dicken's *Tale of Two Cities* followed by: *"It was the time when a riderless horse galloped into Fort Lomax, its saddle bristling with Comanche arrows ..."*

Here we have taken the story away from Revolutionary France to the Wild West: another country and another era. Where the best of times could refer to the opening up of the West to the settlers and the worst of times because of the start of Indian wars. Or from the Indian perspective, it could refer to the last days of freedom for the Plains tribes [best] and the coming of the wagon trains [worst]. Who is telling the story? What happened to the rider? If this idea develops into a completed piece of writing, don't forget to acknowledge where the first line came from but you can see how a good first line can stimulate another train of thought.

Try This Exercise:
In novel writing we need to employ all our senses to achieve a broader and deeper sense of place. We can practise this kind of descriptive writing by this simple exercise:

- Imagine a seascape. Think of the shape of the coastline. Is the beach stony or sandy? Are there any people there? What are they doing? Here we are thinking in terms of the visual but what happens if we broaden our sensual horizons. What is the weather like? What is the time of the day? Can we hear anything? Gulls perhaps, the wind, the scrunch of the sand or shift of the pebbles as we walk? Children's voices? The sound of the sea? Our scene is now more authentic and richer in detail.

- We can go on to think about smells – of salt, sea, candyfloss, suntan-oil, seaweed or sand perhaps. Of the dry smoothness of pebbles, the grittiness of the sand, the feel of the water on our skin. We might taste the salt in the air or the sand in the sandwiches. And we might even wish to introduce a sixth sense in terms of atmosphere and mood.

This exercise can be done with any other setting too. And the really ambitious might like to take themselves back into time and check out the differences that history can make to our scene.

Chapter Twenty

Famous Last Words

This chapter should more accurately be called: *Never name the well from which you will not drink.* In other words, never say you will never do something ... and to go back to that first question asked of writers: *"Do you make any money from it?*

Hopefully *Life-Writes* will have answered those two most common questions asked of writers: *"Where do your ideas come from?"* and *"Do you make any money from it?"* For those who want to go freelance, the message is still as loud and clear as ever: Don't give up the day job, and certainly not before your freelance work or royalties are paying you a living wage.

Life-Writes is the third creative writing book I've written and will most certainly be my last. I've shown where my ideas have come from in the past and present, and revealed a few that will be used in the future. I've drawn on over 20 years of experience as magazine editor, as commissioning editor, novelist and author, freelancer, ghost writer, writing tutor and competition judge – so there can't be anything left to write about. Or can there? I've earned my living (albeit modestly) from freelance writing since 1987 and although it's never been a fortune, since that time I've been a full-time professional writer and it's paid the bills and kept a roof over my head.

Perhaps Simon Whaley summed it all up in his contribution to the 100th issue of *The New Writer*: *"What was I doing back in 1996? Gosh, I was sitting on the tills in Barclay's Bank in Weybridge, dreaming of being a full time writer. And here I am in January 2010, just about to start my sixth year as a full time writer. See, it's worth dreaming isn't it?"*

Most writers, when they start writing with ambition, have very definite ideas about what they will and will not do to get published. Poets shun the popular poetry presses and competitions; short story writers refuse to look at the non-fiction markets or the women's magazines; would-be novelists scorn the romantic fiction publishers ... it doesn't take long, however for everyone to realise that sometimes their writing is better suited to something completely different.

Before we get to this stage, we need to bring some serious focussing into our routine. There is little point in firing off submissions and proposals in a dozen different directions at once, if we've not given any proper thought to how we intend to approach our long-term writing projects. Try to establish a regular pattern for sitting down to write because a writer who shows a marked reluctance to control his or her own writing timetable in the early stages, may discover there are insurmountable difficulties waiting around the corner when it comes to working within deadlines and contracts imposed by others. The focus needed for writing goes beyond filling a blank screen or sheet of paper with words. We have to clearly establish in our own minds what we are attempting to achieve with our writing, and why.

This same focus applies to the construction of the finished typescript; as well as synopses, story-lines, plots and research. Learning to work within self-imposed deadlines are part of the professional writer's craft. Make no mistake – few are born with the natural ability to write really well. The disciplined writer has learned to correct any reoccurring flaws in their work, and is able to recognise when there is a need for a change of style or direction. It doesn't matter what our working methods are (since we all work in different ways), or when and where we apply them – as long as there is a concerted effort to write a set number of words or pages within a fixed time. A literary agent once told me: *"The road to any publisher's office is littered with dead manuscripts of the 'one day I'll get down to it' brigade who failed to learn their craft, or come to terms with the professional attitudes required of today's successful author."*

By being focussed, we don't automatically switch off our brains when we turn off the computer. Even if we're not staring at the screen, our minds will still be ticking over, sifting through information and ideas – which means that we're still 'working' even if we're not actively engaged in writing. Believe it or not, a focussed routine stokes the creative energy that sparks off further bouts of creativity. These 'resting times' often provide the solutions to problems with dialogue and plot, or the elusive line of a poem and because we are actively engaged in the creative process on a conscious level, it means that we are wide open for receiving stimulation from other levels.

These fresh ideas may not necessarily be related to the material we're currently working on, but this is where the Ideas Book comes into its own. Train yourself to record everything as it occurs to you and only discard it when you are absolutely certain that is has no further practical use. In fact, several writers of my acquaintance never throw an Ideas Book away, keeping them as part of their reference section because they can often recycle a really good idea several times over. Some have a collection that goes back years and they can still manage to find an idea or two in those tatty pages!

Other People's Ideas

What, we may ask ourselves, is the difference between using other people's ideas and plagiarism? Firstly, plagiarism is attempting to pass someone else's work off as your own but there is no copyright on ideas, unless these have been developed into a full-length proposal, submitted and recorded. It is, however, quite usual for several people to have the same idea at the same time.

Writers' workshops and the letters page in writing magazines regularly raise the subject of a piece of fiction or an article that one writer has submitted, only to find that a similar piece is published at a later date, credited to someone else. *"How could they have pinched my story?"* is the cry. On the very rare occasion, we have known this to happen but the truth is much simpler … it's all down to those right-brain influences.

It is extremely rare today, for people not to be influenced by the media or social trends. At all times of the day or night, the newspapers, magazines, internet, radio and television intrude on our subconscious thoughts even if we are not consciously tuned in. News items are printed or broadcast in graphic detail and, even though the various television companies, radio stations or newspapers may put a different slant on the reporting, there is little we can do to escape from the coverage. Very often, because we all have a different religious, social or political bias, we will see the same situation, but from various different viewpoints – as we discussed in the mystic mug in Chapter Five.

Fiction editors and competition judges, in particular, can often see where outside stimulus has influenced the choice of subject matter as a surprisingly large proportion of submissions will reflect this in some form or other. There will suddenly be a surge of similar treatments received over a very short period of time. During one competition there was an abnormal number of entries that related to stories set on a tour of the Nile Valley; Egypt was 'in' and quite a lot of stories reflected the increasing popularity for television programmes, Nile cruises and tours. Apart from a few superfluous details, the stories were almost identical in theme and treatment of the subject.

We use other people's ideas when we use research material to give added depth or dimension to a piece of writing. Having watched Crufts on television, one writer wanted to use a particular breed of dog as an antagonist in her story and went to a great deal of trouble to read up on the subject, as well as talking to breeders about the idiosyncrasies of her fictional pampered pet. When the story was submitted, there wasn't a trace of breed description in the entire piece because she'd assimilated the 'facts' into the smooth narrative of the story. The dog simply 'was'. It didn't need describing and yet she'd used all the information she'd been given by the breeder and dog books to create an unconscious picture in the reader's mind of that particular breed.

Having the idea is the first step in fuelling creativity. Immersing yourself with information and stimulating images from other sources will help to develop fresh ideas and different viewpoints. Which means, of course, not using the first idea we think of because hundreds of other people will be doing the same thing, especially if the subject is topical – see Chapter One.

Earlier in Chapter Nineteen we also mentioned 'metatext', which acts as a creative impulse to turn a classic story into something fresh and innovative - here we should avoid the re-telling of Biblical stories in the modern idiom, as this is a common cliché, particularly in competition entries. Sometimes the first line of a popular classic can also be used as an opening (providing due credit is given to the original author) because it states immediately where the story is coming from without a lot of unnecessary preamble. One of the most popular is the extract from T S Eliot's poem *Little Gidding*:

"We shall not cease from exploration
And the end of all our exploring
Will be to arrive where we started
And know the place for the first time."

When trying to come up with an opening for one of my current projects, the esoteric thriller *House of Strange Gods,* I came across a collection of Arthur Machen's short stories and re-discovered the opening line from *The Great Return,* which came in at exactly the right moment where I wanted the novel to start: *"There are strange things lost and forgotten in obscure corners of the newspapers."*

Try not to get bogged down with opening lines and titles in the initial stages because more often than not, they only assume a level of importance when we've finished the first draft. My reason for not being able to get on with a book before the opening is down on paper is due to my own peculiar working methods of creating the entire novel in my head before writing a single word. It is not a method I would encourage anyone else to emulate – but it works for me when writing fiction. When writing non-fiction my working methods are relatively normal, with everything hanging neatly within a pre-established framework.

If we do find that we're being stimulated by other people's ideas we owe it to ourselves to explore as many other avenues of approach as we can. Perhaps we can use 'mapping' to take us to the furthest possible point from the original concept – even reverse the perspective if needs be. Remember it will be the innovative approach that quickens the publisher/editor/competition judges' appreciation of the effort that has gone into the typescript.

Do, however, beware of 'unconscious' plagiarism. I once had a brilliant line appearing in the middle of my text - I even impressed myself! It was natural, it was spontaneous but something about it bothered me. Fortunately, before it went to print I suddenly remembered that it was a line from John Fowles's *The Magus*, which had imprinted itself in my mind. In writing that particular piece of text, Fowles's line was the perfect retort and I'd typed it automatically. In the finish, I got around the problem by using it as a quote because anything else would have been second best.

There is a tremendous satisfaction in completing any poem, short story, play, novel or book but as with every form of saleable writing, we need to be much, much more than just a good writer with an active imagination. We need to understand what is marketable material and be able to be objective about what we are writing. We must act as our own editor and know when and how to cut.

⇨ **The secret is being our own sternest critic but still having faith in our own ability to follow the Creative Pathways – wherever they lead.**

COMPASS
BOOKS

Compass Books, focuses on practical and informative 'how-to' books for writers. Written by experienced authors who also have extensive experience of tutoring at the most popular creative writing workshops, the books offer an insight into the more specialised niches of the publishing game.